THE ESSENTIALS OF

BHAGAVĀN MAHĀVĪR'S PHILOSOPHY

GAṆADHARAVĀDA

LALA SUNDERLAL JAIN RESEARCH SERIES

VOLUME 4

THE ESSENTIALS OF
BHAGAVĀN MAHĀVĪR'S PHILOSOPHY

GAṆADHARAVĀDA

A treatise on the question and answers between eleven Brahmin scholars and Mahāvīr Bhagvān relating to the soul, *karmas, pañca-bhūta,* heaven, hell and salvation, etc.

LATE ACHARYA VIJAY BHUVANBHANUSURI

Translated in English by
PROF. K. RAMAPPA

MOTILAL BANARSIDASS PUBLISHERS
PRIVATE LIMITED • DELHI (INDIA)

*Corrected and Revised Edition: Delhi, **2018***
First Edition: 1989

ISBN : 978-81-208-0677-1 (Cloth)
ISBN : 978-81-208-0678-8 (Paper)

MOTILAL BANARSIDASS
41 U.A. Bungalow Road, Jawahar Nagar, Delhi 110 007
1 B, Jyoti Studio Compound, Kennedy Bridage, Nana Chowk, Mumbai 400 0
203 Royapettah High Road, Mylapore, Chennai 600 004
236, 9th Main III Block, Jayanagar, Bengaluru 560 011
8 Camac Street, Kolkata 700 017
Ashok Rajpath, Patna 800 004
Chowk, Varanasi 221 001

Printed in India

by RP Jain at NAB Printing Unit,
A-44, Naraina Industrial Area, Phase I, New Delhi–110028
and published by JP Jain for Motilal Banarsidass Publishers (P) Ltd.
41 U.A. Bungalow Road, Jawahar Nagar, Delhi-110007

Author—Suvishāl Gachhādipati Acharya Vijay Bhuvanbhanusuri—the dis ciple of Reverend Siddhānt-mahodadhi Acharyadev Vijay Premsooreeshvarji Maharaj

Humbly Dedicated to
Shree Jinbhadragani
Kshamaashraman
Who in his Jināyaṇ named
'Visheshāvashyak Bhāshya'
A marvellous work of Jain
Dravyānuyoga
Included elaborately the discussions
(specified as GAṆADHARVĀDA)
of 11 Brahmin scholars
with Bhagavān Mahāvīr Swami, the
24th Tirthankar in Jainism.

– Author

FOREWORD BY THE TRANSLATOR

The *Ganadharvād* is a philosophical work in which there are profound discussions of eleven salient doctrines. In each of the discussions, one vital *Tattva* is taken up; and Lord Mahāvīr discusses it in great detail and clears the doubt of each Ganadhar with the result that each Ganadhar is fully convinced of the truth of the Lord's argument and becomes his disciple. The eleven Ganadhars are: 1) Indrabhuti – his doubt is regarding the existence of the soul; 2) Agnibhuti – his doubt is regarding *Karmas;* 3) Vayubhuti – his doubt is whether the body itself is the *Jiva* or whether it is different from the *Jiva*; 4) Vyakta – his doubt is whether the five material elements are real or unreal; 5) Sudharma – his doubt is whether the *Jiva* will be of the same kind or different in the next birth; 6) Mandit – his doubt is regarding bondage; 7) Mauryaputra – his doubt is regarding the existence of heaven; 8) Akampit – his doubt is whether hell is real; 9) Achalbhrata – his doubt is regarding the existence of *Punya* and *Pāpa;* 10) Metarya – his doubt is regarding the existence of the other world; 11) Prabhas – his doubt is regarding *Mokṣa.*

The doubts of the eleven Ganadhars are of a crucial nature and Lord Mahāvīr by means of convincing arguments and logical discussions of vital principles clears the doubts of the Ganadhars and inspires them to become his followers. This is the subject matter of the book.

As a work dealing with profound philosophical discussions, it resembles the great Dialogues of Plato; in its style and in the techniques of communication employed. The author of The Ganadharvād, the Revered Gurumaharaj, Acharya Sri Bhuvanbhanusurishvarji Maharaj, is a scriptural scholar of outstanding excellence and astounding mastery. His greatness as a writer is evident from the fact that he expounds and establishes, in the clearest terms possible, the most difficult and complicated metaphysical and philosophical concepts and doctrines. His examples and illustrations are so clear, so lucid, so pointed and so appropriate that they enable even lay readers to comprehend clearly and correctly the subtleties and complexities of the philosophical and metaphysical theories discussed. Hegel says: "Logic might have been defined as the science of thought and of its laws and characteristic forms. But thought as thought constitutes only the general medium, or qualifying circumstance, which renders the idea distinctively logical. If we identify the idea with thought, thought must not be taken in the sense of a method or form but in the sense of the self-developing totality of its laws and peculiar terms. These laws are the work of thought itself and not a fact which it finds and must submit to." This definition of logic given by the great German philosopher helps us to understand the incisive intellectual analysis of abstract theories that we find in the book. The great Guru Maharaj presents the arguments of the Lord in an absolutely logical and therefore, convincing manner.

Jainism is not, as some make it out to be, a modern religion which, in their view, arose, not as a natural philosophical growth but as a reaction against the corruptions that had crept into the Vedic religion. Of course, Jainism rejects the authority of the Vedas and dismisses some systems of philosophy as founded on Ekāntavād, a single point of view.

All the great Jain scholars who have written on Jainism concede that the Anekāntavād (the multiple point of view) expounded by Jain philosophers and methods of acquiring knowledge. The Syādvād or the Saptabhangi developed by the Jain thinkers, views reality from seven points of view, namely:

1) In some aspect it is existent (Real) (*Syāt asti*)
2) In some aspect it is non-existent (Unreal) (*Syāt nāsti*)
3) In some aspect it is existent and non-existent (*Syāt asti nāsti*)
4) In some aspect it is inexpressible (*Syāt avaktavyaḥ*)
5) In some aspect it is existent and is inexpressible (*Syāt asti ca avaktavyaḥ*)
6) In some aspect it is non-existent and is inexpressible (*Syāt nāsti ca avaktavyaḥ*)
7) In some aspect it is existent, non-existent and is inexpressible (*Syāt asti ca nāsti ca avaktavyaḥ*)

This method of looking at reality from the seven points of view, according to Jain philosophers helps us to acquire a composite and complete view of the reality. The Jain philosophical enquiry is based on this method and so it is absolutely logical. Prof. Hiriyanna says, "The Jainas think that reality is so complex in its structure that while everyone of these views is true as far as it goes none is completely so." So, Jain thinkers try to describe reality from seven points of view known as Saptabhangi. Moreover, Jain philosophers believe that we must view reality not only in a relative sense but also in relation to Material, Place, Time and State. This philosophical method of enquiry called Saptabhangi is a remarkable contribution of the Jain philosophers to the development of our philosophic awareness. The great Guru Maharaj, the author of the book, presents the arguments from the *Anekāntavād* point of view and establishes various theories and doctrines. "To understand the exact significance of this doctrine, it is necessary to know the conditions, under which it was formulated. There was then, on the one hand, the Upanishadic view that being alone was true; and on the other, the view, also mentioned in the Upanishads, but with disapproval that non-being was the ultimate truth. Both these views, according to Jainism are only partially true and each becomes a dogma as soon as it is understood to represent the whole truth about reality"– Prof. Hiriyanna.

Jainism believes that the universe is made up of two ultimate substances, namely the *Jiva* (that which is conscious) and the *Ajiva* (that which lacks consciousness). The *Ajiva* is of five kinds, namely, the *Dharmastikay,* the *Adharmastikay,* the *Akashastikay,* the *Pudgalastikay,* and *Kala* (or Time). *Kala* is not an Astikay. The Jivas are infinite in number but they are of two broad kinds, namely 1) The *Mukta Jivas* (those that have attained an absolute freedom from all bondages of *Karmas)* and 2) The *Samsari Jivas* (those that are in the *samsār).* According to Jainism, it is in the hands of the *Jiva* to get rid of the bondage of *Karmas* and to attain *Mokṣa. Karmas* have been in the soul from time immemorial and they can be destroyed by means of *Samvar* and *Nirjarā. Samvar* means blocking the six influxes or channels through which Karmas enter the soul. Just as the well is purified by chemicals, the Karmas in the soul can be destroyed by means of *Nirjarā* or spiritual austerities and thus the soul can become the supreme Soul. In other words, man is God in the making. This reminds us of Bergson's philosophy of creative evolution. Bergson believed that Life Force or Elan

Vital compels all individuals to rise to higher and higher levels of refinement, towards perfection.

Jainism lays a special emphasis on the importance of ethical excellence. It has expounded five great principles of conduct, namely 1) *Ahimsa* (non-violence), 2) *Satya* (speaking the truth), 3) *Asteya* (non stealing), 4) *Brahmacharya* (Celibacy), 5) *Aparigraha* (non-attachment). The Jain Dharma also has three gems (the Ratna-traya): 1) *Samyag Jñan* (the right knowledge), 2) *Samyag Darshan* (the right faith), and 3) *Samyag Charitra* (the right conduct). The Jain Dharma prescribes minor vows *(Anuvratas)* for householders and major vows *(Mahavratas)* for Sadhus and Sadhvis.

The Jain philosophers of ancient times explored the universe by means of their extra-ordinary and supramental powers of perception in conformity with Anekāntavād and expounded their theories of the universe. The Jain philosophy has its roots in such springs of wisdom as Purvas and Agamas. Prof. Hiriyanna says, "The half-hearted character of the Jaina enquiry is reflected in the sevenfold mode of predication (*Saptabhangi*) which stops at giving us the several partial views together without attempting to overcome the opposition in them by a proper synthesis." But the Jain thinkers assert that *Syādvād* is neither *Samshayavād* (scepticism) nor *Anishchyavād* (indecision) but that it is a multidimensional approach to reality and that this method, also called Anekāntavād, attempts to see, to know and to understand reality as in itself it really is.

Jainism has a vast treasure of literature comprising outstanding works on philosophy, metaphysics, logic, astronomy, ethics, and various other subjects besides pure literature comprising poems, prose-works and fiction.

The great Guru Maharaj, Acharya Sri Vijay Bhuvanbhanu-surishvarji Maharaj has mastered the entire philosophy of Jainism and has in this short book, expounded the essentials of Jain philosophy.

The work of translating this book into English has been an enlightening experience for me, especially because at every step the Gurudev read the manuscript, suggested improvements and gave the necessary guidance and recast the matter.

I am sure that this work will be a precious addition to the existing philosophical knowledge in English because it abounds in original insights, scholarly interpretations and masterly expositions of philosophical and metaphysical theories.

No. 602, III Cross,
Hanumantha Nagar,
Bangalore-560 019

K. RAMAPPA

जयतु सर्वज्ञ-शासनम्

PREFACE

In the *shivir* held in the summer vacation in 1963 A.C. at Abu—Achalgad College – the participants including those of the previous *shivir* requested Acharyadev Vijay Bhuvanbhanu-surishvarji Maharaj to preach and expound the essentials of the Jain philosophy of higher level. The Revered Acharyadev in order to fulfil their desire compiled the *Ganadharavad* from *Jain Agamas* in which the discussions between Bhagavān Mahāvīr and eleven brahmin scholars are described in detail. The discussions relate to souls, karmas, the next birth, the bondages, the reality of the world, heaven, hell and salvation etc. The Gurudev explained and preached all these ideas to the students in a lucid and interesting manner. The *Ganadharavad* was published as a part of the Gujarati book *Jain Dharmano Saral Parichay* (An Easy Introduction to the Jain Dharma). Later, a Hindi version of the book was also published. Now, its English version is being published under the title "*The Essentials of Bhagavān Mahāvīr's Philosophy.*"

Some may desire to know what is the need and importance of the *Ganadharavad*? The answer to this question is that now-a-days such illogical beliefs as the following are prevalent, and they have to be corrected:

(1) Some believe that there is no such independent substance called the soul different from the body; because from birth to death what is concretely perceptible is the body, and so they say: "Why should we then believe in the invisible soul when all actions and events are going on ceaselessly as if without the soul?" They may ask the question: "How do happiness and sorrow arise?" and their answer to this question is that everything occurs by chance.

(2) Another belief of these people is that there is no such thing as the next birth, because no dead man has returned

from the other world and given any information about it; nor has anyone shown any affection for his previous relatives.

(3) A third belief of these people is that such entities as Karmas, destiny and fortune do not exist because they are not visible. Moreover, many religious-minded people, though earning good fortune are seen to be afflicted with worries. Then where is the question of the existence of good fortune?

(4) A fourth belief of these people is that there is no such place as heaven or hell. They think that people, knowing the existence of hell would not have committed sins that lead to hell, if hell really existed.

(5) Their fifth belief is that the world which is full of unevenness and strangeness is unreal and void like a dream.

But that all these beliefs are false and illusory can be comprehended from the discussions that took place between the Tirthankar Bhagavān Mahāvīr Swami and the eleven Brahmin scholars relating to souls, Karmas, body itself possessing consciousness, illusoriness of the whole world, heaven, hell, salvation etc. Hence we feel that if these discussions founded on reasoning are presented before them, their false beliefs would be dispelled, and they would be impressed with the truth of philosophy. Here, we give some valuable opinions of some great men and some ideas occurring in the ancient scriptures.

I. *The opinions of western scholars about the Jain Dharma :*

I like the doctrines of Jainism greatly. If I were to be reborn, I wish to be born as a Jain.

George Bernard Shaw

The Jain dharma is absolutely different and independent from the Hindu dharma.

Max Muller

The Jain dharma has not borrowed ideas from other religions, nor is it an imitation of other religions.

Dr. Herman Jacobi

II. *The opinions of the Indian scholars about the Jain Dharma :*

If there is a religion which is ancient, true and supremely sound, it is the Jain dharma.

Yogi Sivanand Paramhamsa

The modern research in history has proved that the Jain dharma existed even before Brahminism or the Hindu dharma.

Justice Rangnekar

Lord Mahāvīr communicated the message that dharma is only the truth. It is realy significant that this message has captivated the whole country.

Rabindranath Tagore

We can attain absolute serenity by following the path shown by Mahavir. On account of its philosophy of non-violence, the Jain dharma is worthy of becoming the religion of the world.

Dr. Rajendra Prasad

The Tirthankars are given prominence and honour even in the Yajuraveda. The Jain dharma has been in existence from time immemorial.

Dr. Radhakrishnan

The true and sublime message of Mahavir inspires in us the lofty emotion of universal amity as if through the cry of a 'Conch-Shell'

Sir Akbar Hydari

I very much like the subtler aspects of the Jain philosophical doctrines.

Mohammed Hafiz Sayed

According to the *Syadvad,* we cannot attain a complete knowledge of an object unless we view it from various points of view. The *syadvad* teaches us how we should look at the universe.

Prof. Anandshankar Dharuva

In the end, I hope that those who wish their precious human birth to attain a higher spiritual level will be amply benefitted by this book.

36, Kalikund Society,
Dholka
(Ahmedabad)
Gujarat

Kumarpal V. Shah

OM ARHAM NAMAH

Introduction of Shri Prakashchand Samdaria.

Human life is the most valuable asset of fortunate beings. Infinite knowledge, power, riches, supreme godliness and humility are within the reach of man and man alone. If man practises selflessness, altruism and progress towards self-realization, besides working for the upliftment of humanity, his fame and glory are bound to spread in all directions. Shri Prakashchand Samdaria son of Shri Kanmalji Samdaria of Nagaur, Rajasthan had led such a simple and exemplary life and from his very childhood he was drawn towards noble and pious activities. His parents had duly contributed their share in bringing up a cultured child.

He never missed any oppurtunity of paying reverence to Sadhus and Sadhvis and would be immensely pleased and his heart would be overwhelmed with joy and bliss.

Compassion and love for Godliness and goodliness, are indeed of much greater value than riches and degrees. Shri Prakashchand Samdaria was a philanthropist in the true sense of the term. Besides inspiring people to establish themselves in pious deeds, during his life time he himself carried out innumerable religious and social activities and had great respect for all those who served the Jinashasana and worked for the welfare of all groups of people.

Though a prestigious personality in the society, he was never proud of his wealth, riches and status. With immense devotion and unparalleled dedication he whole-heartedly donated for the reconstruction of Jain temples, constructed and established by great, devoted Shrimants and Acharyas of olden times. To materialize splendid projects of the construction of Jain temples and others, he gave valuable service in many places of India in cash and kind and in true terms led a glorious life.

Similarly his valuable contribution in the publication of almanacs (Panchanga) by Shri Arunodaya foundation deserve a special mention and he shall be remembered for his constructive and generous contribution, as long as such noble deeds are undertaken by pious people.

His wife Smt. Kamalkanwar Devi has succeeded him in all respects and has kept the lamp of goodness and charity burning. She has given financial assistance for publication of this book. Thus Prakashchandji served the Jinashasana elegantly and it is our turn now to pray for his soul to rest in peace and hope that his family follows his foot-steps with courage and conviction and serve the mighty Jinashasana.

Smt. Dhankanwar Kanmalji Samadaria, mother of Prakashchandji. She performed two *UPADHYAN* austerity with the penance of Navpad Āyambil oli, Akshayanidhi, Gnānpanchami, Meru Jerash, Vish-sthānak oli etc.

This book has been published with best compliments from Smt. Kamlabai Prakashcandji Samdaria

CONTENTS

1
THE DOUBT REGARDING THE EXISTENCE OF THE SOUL

Bhagavān Shri Mahāvīr Paramatma, the Lord of the three worlds, lived his final life in this world two thousand five hundred years ago. He embodied the spirit of renunciation even from his birth and he also knew for certain that in this last birth he would attain salvation (*Mokṣa*) at the end; yet, he renounced worldly life and accepted life-long vows of non-violence etc. He became an *Anagar* (Ascetic) at the age of thirty on the 10th day of the dark fortnight of Margashirsh (Kartik according to the Gujarati calculations). On that day he adopted Sadhu-dharma and became a Muni, impelled by his extraordinary spiritual awareness. But what was the reason for this? The foremost duty of any human being is to adopt the path of sinless conduct (*Charitra-dharma*) and only this path can lead human beings to '*Mokṣa*.' As soon as he became a Muni, he attained the fourth knowledge (*Atma Pratyaksha* = direct perception of others' minds) *Manah-paryay-Jñān* (an extraordinary power of perceiving the mental processes of other *Panchendriya Jivas* i.e. *jivas* with five senses). As a rule every Tirthankar even while in the mother's womb possesses three kinds of knowledge, namely *Mati-jñān* (perception by senses); *Shruta-jñān* (knowledge of scriptures and *Avadhi-jñān* (extrasensory perception). The fourth kind of perception *Manah-paryay-jñān*, arises in him when he renounces wordly relations and possessions and accepts the vows of asceticism.

After accepting the *Charitra-dharma*, Lord Mahāvīr carried out the severest spiritual austerities and penances for twelve and a half years. Moreover, he always used to remain in *Kayotsarg* (a standing, steady posture of the body for deep meditation). During that period he endured terrible impediments caused by human beings, animals and celestial beings, the severe hardships of cold and heat etc. How long did he sleep during those twelve and a half years? Not a minute of lying down on the ground but simply drowsing, that too, during the whole period of twelve years only for one *Muhurt*, i.e. for 48 minutes. Oh! What an extraordinary kind of awareness!

What an extraordinary spiritual yearning! The poet says:

साडा बार वरस जिन उत्तम पीरजी भूमि न ठाया हो,
घोर तप केवल ळह्या तेहना पद्मविजय नमे पाया ॥

"Throughout the twelve and a half years the loftiest Lord Mahāvīr did not at all lie down on the ground (earth). (The poet) Padmavijay bows to the feet of Lord Mahāvīr, the greatest of the *Vitarags* (those who have conquered all internal enemies like attachments, hatred etc.,) who attained *Kevaljñān* (infinite perception) by means of severe penances."

The Lord whose pure and perfect soul had attained absolute purity, possessed such virtues as complete freedom from illusion, total indifference to dependence on and relation with animate and inanimate objects, complete non-indulgence in worldly pleasures, absolute purity, total absence of bondage. He had an absolute restraint over the senses and the mind, total freedom from all attachments and hatred. Owing to the absence of even the least affection, his senses turned inwards to the absolute, unadulterated form of the soul, and he developed extreme spiritual awareness and equanimity. He attained *Kevaljñān* (i.e. omniscience) on the evening of the 10th day of the bright fortnight of Vaishakh on the bank of the river Rijuvaluka; and thus he attained a complete perception of the entire cosmos comprising *Lokākāsh* and *Alokākāsh* and all other objects.

What are the objects that can be perceived by one who has attained omniscience (*Kevaljñān*) ? Now, the Lord became omniscient and he therefore, could clearly and directly see all souls and all *Pudgals* (inanimate material substances); and all their infinite modifications (transformations), recurring through all the three phases of time. He could perceive the whole cosmos, of the past, the present, and the future, simultaneously. He could see and know directly just as one can see *myrobalan* fruit, placed on his palm, all the infinite souls that attained salvation in the beginningless past and all the countless souls that will attain salvation in the infinite future which are outnumbered by the existing souls in a

Nigod (the *Sadharan Vanaspatya-Kay*), infinite times. Although souls attaining salvation are countless and infinite in number, they are very few in comparison with the Nigod souls. The souls in the *Nigod* will ever remain infinite- fold more in proportion to the liberated souls. In each and every soul there exist countless subtle molecular parts (*pradeshas*) and on each of them infinite Karmic multitudes (*Karma-skandhas*) are stuck. In each of these *Karma-skandhas* there are infinite number of Karmic subtle atoms (*Paramanus*). Each such atom has undergone an infinite number of *Bhavas* (modifications) in the infinite time. The modifications exist in all states and in all times. According to this mathematical calculation all souls (conscious animate beings) and *Ajivas* (inert, inanimate substances) possess such infinite number of modifications. The omniscience Bhagavān Lord Mahāvīr Paramatma visualizes and knows all these modifications and transformations in their forms both, common and uncommon (individual). The omniscients (*Kevaljñānis*) perceive directly the distinctive nature of the minutest karmas and also of the pure and liberated formless souls as well as the peculiar and polluted natures of the souls bound by subtle karma. Only those who firmly believe in these peculiarities, as visualized by the omniscients can have deep interest in carrying out His commands and in rendering worship and devotion to Him.

What the poet says about this is quite proper:

केवली-निरखित सूक्ष्म अरुपी ते जेहने चित्त पसीयो रे,
जिन उत्तमपद पद्मनी सेवा, करवामा धणुं रसियो रे ॥

After attaining omniscience of the above-mentioned nature, Bhagavān Lord Mahāvīr Swami arrived at the Mahasen Garden, near the City of Apāpa. The divine beings constructed a magnificent *Samavasaran* (a preaching platform) with three castles. The divine beings, human beings and animals arrived there. Indra himself entreats the Paramatman to deliver a religious sermon.

सुरपति आया वंदनकाज भगते भराणा रे हो, करे जिन पूजना रे,
जिनजी तुं भवजल तार प्रभुजी तुं पार उतार,
सरस सुधाशी रेहो, देइ अम देशना रे ॥

(Indra, the King of gods arrived at the *Samavasaran*; offered his heartfelt salutations to Him and worshipped Him with overflowing devotion. He said, "O Lord! You have crossed the ocean of world. Guide us also to cross that boundless ocean; lift us out of it. Kindly bestow upon us the benefaction of being delighted and elevated spiritually by your enlightened and nectarlike utterances that can bring us the supreme serenity and felicity."

Visualize this situation as if it existed before you, with a devout heart. Imagine that we have reached this *samavasaran*. Imagine that we are also witnessing that magnificent spectacle, that Almighty Lord, and that we are also bathing in that boundless ocean of felicity and serenity. If we imagine ourselves there, we can visualize all that as if it is occurring before our eyes, and we are thus benefitted immensely. We can destroy our Karmas and our souls will attain purity and elevation.

The Eleven Brahmins – The future *Ganadhars*– A certain wealthy brahmin by name Somil had arranged a Yajna (a sacrifice) in the city of Apāpa. He had invited eleven learned brahmins who had mastered the Vedas and who were well-versed in fourteen Vidyas or intellectual accomplishments. Each of them had hundreds of pupils with him. Everyone of the brahmins presumed himself to be an omniscient but their knowledge was incomplete since each of them had doubts regarding different doctrines which arose from the contradictory statements in the Vedas. However, strangely enough they committed the mistake of presuming themselves to be omniscients. What was the cause for this blunder? They had acquired knowledge of various Vidyās with extraordinary industry and diligence. They had attained mastery over many *Shastras* (Scriptural Texts). They had a profound self-confidence. Yet they had not understood the derivation and the full meaning of the word *Sarvajñata* or omniscience or they had only a vague idea of what it meant; so, they believed that they were omniscient.

The Eleven Doubts of the eleven brahmins:

(1) Indrabhuti Gautam had a doubt regarding the soul. His doubt was this: "In this universe, is there an entity called *Atma* (the Soul) which is independent and eternal?" (2) Agnibhuti Gautam, another scholar, had a doubt regarding *Karma*. His doubt was whether everything that happened was

only the soul's doing or according to *karma.* Is there such an entity as *Karma?* (3) Vayubhuti Gautam had this doubt: "Is this body itself the soul or is the soul different from the body?" These three Brahmins were brothers and each of them had five hundred pupils. (4) The scholar by name Vyakta had a doubt regarding the five elements. His doubt was this: "There are the five material elements, namely *Prithvi* (earth), *Ap* (water), *Tejas* (fire), *Vayu* (air) and *Akash* (Vacuum-space). Are these real or unreal and illusory like a dream?" (5) Sudharma's doubt was this: "Is the soul in the next birth the same kind as in this birth or different?" These two scholars had five hundred pupils each. (6) Mandit, another brahmin, had a doubt regarding bondage. His doubt was this: "Is the soul for ever pure, enlightened and free from that bondage by means of proper endeavours?" (7) Mauryaputra had a doubt regarding celestial beings. His doubt was this: "Is there a place called Heaven at all?" Each of these two scholars had three hundred and fifty pupils. (8) In the same manner, Akampit had a doubt regarding the existence of hell. (9) Achalbhrata had a doubt regarding *punya* or good actions. His doubt was this: "Why should we believe in both good luck and bad luck? Let there be one." (10) Metarya had a doubt regarding the existence of the next birth and (11) The scholar by name Prabhas had a doubt regarding salvation, *Mokṣa.* His doubt was this: "Is there a definite state called *Mokṣa*? Does the soul attain a state of eternal, boundless and pure happiness? Is the *jiva* completely destroyed or annihilated after its *samsār* is completed?" Each of these scholars had three hundred pupils.

The Eleven Ganadhars and their Doubts :

No.	Name of the Ganadhar	His doubt
1.	Indrabhuti	His doubt was regarding the existence of soul.
2.	Agnibhuti	His doubt was regarding *Karmas.*
3.	Vayubhuti	His doubt was whether the body itself is the *jiva* or whether it is different from *jiva.*

4.	Vyakta	His doubt was whether the five elements were real or unreal like a dream.
5.	Sudharma	His doubt was whether the *jiva* will be of the same kind or of a different kind in the next birth.
6.	Mandit	His doubt was regarding bondage.
7.	Mauryaputra	His doubt was regarding the existence of Heaven.
8.	Akampit	His doubt was whether hell was real.
9.	Achalbhrata	His doubt was regarding the existence of good luck and bad luck.
10.	Metarya	His doubt was regarding the existence of the next birth.
11.	Prabhas	His doubt was regarding *Mokṣa.*

These eleven Brahmins and their pupils numbering 4400 were participating in the Yajna (ceremony). From what people were saying and from their movements, they understood that some omniscient one had arrived there.

The Pride of Indrabhuti: On the other side, the brahmins noticed celestial beings descending from the sky to earth. They could not contain their joy and elation. They exclaimed triumphantly, "Oh! Look up! How tremendously efficacious our Yajna is. It has compelled even deities to come down to earth." But when Indrabhuti noticed that those deities were not coming to the Yajna and that they were proceeding in the sky further without stopping and descending there, he was greatly disappointed. He thought with disappointment "Ah! these heavenly beings are ignorant. Why have they fallen into this illusion? Neglecting the sacred waters of the Ganga, like crows, they are proceeding to drink foul and polluted water somewhere else! Who has become a new *Sarvajña*?" Note the strangeness of this situation: It is surprising that Indrabhuti who did not even know who had become a new omniscient presumed himself to be a *Sarvajña,* i.e. an omniscient one. Not only this; when we cannot attain something that is good and beneficial we condemn it just as the fox who could not reach the grapes saying, "The grapes are sour." Jealousy is a bugbear. Indrabhuti thinks, "Oh! only a fool can be deceived by hypocrites but these are celestial beings. They are called *Vibudhs* (those who have attained awakening) and even they have been deceived. But no! These deities may not be really heavenly beings. They must be pretenders like that false *sarvajña."* They are false deities just as he is a false *sarvajña.* He tried to explain the situation to himself thus and yet he could not forget the new omniscient one. He could not bear to hear the name of another *Sarvajña* apart from himself. It is astonishing that he forgot the ten Brahmin *sarvajñas* accompanying him.

That was an age in which great scholars had scriptural knowledge at the tip of their tongue. Here, by means of strenuous efforts, Indrabhuti had attained mastery over various branches of Vidyas, knowledge, and had defeated reputed scholars. In spite of that, under the pride born of *Mithyatva* (false faith) he became angry and thought: "Only one sun exists in the world. Only one sword can exist in a scabbard. Only one lion can stay in a cave. In the same manner, there can be only one *sarvajña* i.e. one omniscient in the world. I cannot bear with the idea that there can be another Sarvajña." How full of resentment he was! What a pitiable intolerance! He did not tolerate even the existence of another omniscient one. Of course, he was aware of the fact that there were with him ten learned Brahmins who deemed themselves to be omniscient, but he did not give them any importance. Why did he ignore them? Say, those ten brahmins deemed Indrabhuti to be superior to them and venerable. They used to follow him as their leader. So it means that man thirsts only for prestige and honour. After a person falls into the snares of honour and prestige, if he himself cannot get honour, he will be greatly disappointed; and even if the opponent possesses infinite virtues, he would not feel happy; and he would not treat him with friendliness or love. On the contrary, he would be troubled by jealousy and hatred.

The glorification of the Lord by the people: Preparation for a debate by Indrabhuti. People were returning from the

Samavasaran after having offered their salutations to Lord Mahāvīr. Indrabhuti sarcastically asks them: "Have you come after seeing that sarvajña? What kind of sarvajña is he?" The Lord was countless times more radiant and more beautiful than the heavenly beings residing in the heaven called *Anuttarviman* (the uppermost heaven). The trumpets called *Devdundubhis* blown by the divine beings, the shower of divine flowers, the whisks, *Ashta-Pratiharya* i.e. the eight splendid paraphernalia such as the sublime and radiant halo of light – all had been witnessed by the people. The Lord's voice possessed the thirty-five sublime virtues. They were returning after being delighted with the sight of those splendid things. Therefore, their hearts were over-flowing with joy, and they had been fascinated by the sight. How could they describe in words all that splendour? So the people said: "Even if all the inhabitants in the three worlds keep enumerating the infinite virtues of the supreme Lord for countless millennia, his virtues will ever remain beyond comprehension. If mathematical calculation could go beyond a *parardha*, and if the life span (of one who takes up such calculation) is endless, then only all the virtues of the Lord can be completely enumerated." How could Indrabhuti tolerate this praise of the Lord? He felt shocked and said: "Oh! He has deceived these people also. I will not delay even a moment. I will at once go to Him and expose his arrogance and deception by defeating him in a debate with him. The wind which has blown away mighty elephants will not find it difficult to blow away a small flake of cotton. When I have routed the greatest scholars of the world, how could he escape from me? When I have crushed the oil out of every grain of sesame, how could this grain escape my notice? No worry, it is a very easy thing for me to defeat him. When I have defeated countless scholars and created a famine (scarcity) of scholars, in which village had this scholar hidden himself all these days? Whatever it may be, I shall have to go there."

Thinking thus, he made preparations to see the Lord. But Agnibhuti came to know of it and said, "where is the need for your going there? Is it necessary to send the 'Airavat', i.e. the elephant of Indra to pull out a lotus strand? Kindly remain here. I will go and defeat him." Indrabhuti said, "Oh! Not only you, but any pupil of mine can defeat him, but I cannot bear to hear another person being glorified as an omnicient one. Therefore, I myself will go. I cannot have peace of mind until I defeat him. A woman might have safeguarded her chastity for one hundred years but if she loses her chastity once, she is no more chaste. In the same manner, if there exists even one single disputant who is not conquered by me, it is a blow to my honour and prestige."

Indrabhuti got ready to meet the Lord. He marked a dozen '*Tilaks*', auspicious marks on his body, head and forehead etc. He put on radiant silk garments and also wore a sacred thread made of pure gold. He set off followed by his five hundred pupils. Some carried a mendicant's bowl in their hands; some carried holy 'Durva' grass in their hands. Indrabhuti was bubbling with self-confidence. "Is there any branch of *vidya* (knowledge) which I have not mastered? I have studied and mastered grammar, literature, logic, the *Vedas,* astrology etc. In all these branches of knowledge I have worked indefatigably. The scholars of the territory of Lat Desh ran away defeated by me. I heaped disgrace on the Dravidian scholars. The scholars of Telang were utterly crushed like sesame by me. I simply crushed the scholars of Gurjara beyond recognition". What is all this? Was it a sort of self-assessment or a preparation to submit to the unexpected show of the omnicients genius? Indrabhuti went thinking thus and he reached the divine *samavasaran* and stood before the Lord.

Indrabhuti is shocked at the sight of the Lord: When he looked up, what did he see? He saw unrivalled, unparalleled, extra-ordinary, peerless, matchless, inestimable, incomputable supreme Lord Mahāvīr, the last Tirthankar and the supreme spiritual head of the three worlds shining resplendent with his incomparable, unique and indescribable and unimaginable beauty and splendour. Indras were waving '*Chamars*' (a sort of whisks). The heavenly nymphs kept watching him with unwinking eyes. Indrabhuti was astonished at the very sight of this Lord. He thought, "Who is he?" He tried to recognise him. "Can he be Lord Vishnu? No, Lord Vishnu has a blue complexion but this one has a radiant and golden complexion. His body is shining like gold. Can he be Brahma? But brahma is old while this one is young. Can he be Lord Shankar? But Shankar smears his body with holy ash;

and has a cobra around his hand and neck. But this one does not have those things. Can he be the Meru mountain? No: The Meru mountain is hard whereas his body is tender and soft like butter-mass. He cannot be even the sun because the sun burns the eyes of those who see it whereas the sight of this one brings coolness to the eyes of the beholders. Perhaps this may be the moon. Of course, the light of the moon is pleasant and bright but he cannot be the moon. The moon has a black spot on it while he is utterly spotless. Then who can he be?" Indrabhuti tried his best to find out who the man was and for this purpose he reviewed mentally all the religions, philosophies and scriptures he had mastered. Then he at once found out that he must be the twenty-fourth Tirthankar glorified by the Jains, one who was free from all vices and defects and one who embodied infinite virtues. Of course, he did find out who he was; but he was confounded. "Oh! Have I to carry out a debate with him?"

Mithyatva or False Faith is a Common Thing:– Indrabhuti of course recognised the Lord. So it was time for him to accept him as an authority. Then why delay? What was the cause for a delay in getting rid of false faith? By good luck, he met the Lord Tirthankar but he could not understand him fully until his mind acquired the proper mental attitude. If a man owing to any error of the previous birth is bound by the *Mithyatva mohaniya karma*, what would be his condition when that karma ripens and produces its effects? When does a man have to go far to gather this *Mithyatva mohaniya karma*? If one doubts the words of the omniscient one, if one disbelieves the unshakeable words of the Paramatma under the pretext of the change of place and time and scientific developments, the *Mithyatva* will at once cling to the soul. We should not lose faith in our dharma, and comdemn it, fascinated by the apparent attraction of *Mithyatva*, and its arguments. If we condemn or undermine the Sangha or sadhus or the fellow-members of our faith and if we condemn and criticise adversely austerities and the spirit of renunciation, we gather this *karma*.

Indrabhuti had been till then in the snares of *Mithyatva*. Therefore though he was in the presence of the supreme Lord possessing infinite virtues, he could not seek his shelter and accept his refuge. He entertained fears. He experienced repentance: "I think I have fallen into some snares. I have come to carry out a debate with this Supreme Lord who is seated on a golden throne studded with diamonds, and who is honoured and worshipped by countless heavenly beings. What would I lose if I can not defeat him? This is nothing but foolishness on my part. I am going to lose the previous place of my honour and prestige; just as a foolish person tries to destroy his palace for the sake of a nail." Think over this. Though Indrabhuti was haughty, he had the wisdom to recognise the abilities and merits of the opponent. Indrabhuti himself says, "He is the last Thirthankar, the one who is absolutely spotless. Oh! What a fool I am in thinking of defeating the incarnation of Lord Ishvar?" Indrabhuti had not yet attained the Jin-Shasan. He had not yet understood the Jain doctrines. He had not yet developed faith in the Jain Dharma, still he understood the circumstances properly and had the power of self criticism and realising his own foolishness, Why? He had the power of discrimination. Yet, it is wonderful that he did not seek the refuge of such a Lord. What kind of heart had he? He thought "What has happened? What can be done? Where shall I go? May god Shiva safeguard my fame and prestige". This is the effect of *Mithyatva*. Though he was in the presence of the supreme world-preceptor, the incarnation of God, yet, he could not seek his refuge, but thought of finding his refuge in Shiva! His prayer for refuge goes to Shiva.

Again he began building castles in the air like a foolish *Shekhchilli*. There is a proverb: 'God helps those who help themselves'. So, he thought 'If I can defeat him using my vast scriptural knowledge, I will become famous in the three worlds. Oh! and then what will be my status, prestige and my greatness? They are indescribable.' What kind of a whim is this?

Yet, this thinking is true. Indrabhuti was going to achieve such a marvellous victory over illusion and ignorance at the hands of the Lord and was going to attain prestige in the three worlds, but all that would happen only when once he was defeated at the hands of the Lord. Where does our victory lie? Does it lie in our defeat at the hands of the enlightened preceptor or does it lie in our defeating the preceptor? "I am not at all defeated. He has fooled me only in his own castle and in the presence of his own followers. Can any importance be attached to such a victory?" If he had thought like this, and feigned baselessly he could not have attained a real victory over his illusion. Therefore, specially in this modern age of decline *(kaliyuga)* we should refrain from revealing our external prudence in the presence of spiritual heads. We should admit our defects in the presence of elderly people and even if we do not have defects, we should say, "I have forgotten the right path. I have gone astray. So kindly pardon me. Oh! Lord". In this kind of humbleness lies the fruitfulness of this valuable human birth.

Meanwhile, the omniscient Shri Vardhaman Svami, said with a voice which was solemn like an ocean and sweet like nectar: "O Indrabhuti Gautam! You have come, I believe, without any trouble". The Lord possessing infinite knowledge knew what effect this first medicine, namely, these assuring words, would produce on the soul of Indrabhuti and what sort of second medicine would be necessary. Indrabhuti thought, "Ah! He even knows my name. Why not? In the three worlds, is there anyone who does not know my name and calls me by my name. If he mentions the doubt lying in my heart, I would deem him a true omniscient one." The supreme Lord Shraman Bhagavān Mahāvīr Parmatma possesses infinite knowledge. Nothing is unknown to him. Then what to talk of this doubt? So suddenly he said "Oh Indrabhuti Gautam! Why do you doubt the existence of the *jivas* in this world thinking 'Is there in this world any substance like *jiva* or not?' But, why don't you think and rightly understand the statements in the Vedas." The Lord recited the actual wording of the Vedic sentences.

"विज्ञानधन एव एतेभ्यो भुतेभ्यः समुत्थाय तान्येवानुविनश्यति न प्रेत्यसंज्ञास्तीति" ।।

Ah! How sublime was the voice of the Lord when he recited the statements from the Vedas. His voice was like the voice produced by the churning of the ocean. It was like the voice of the mighty floods of the Ganga. It was like the first voice of the creator Brahma. What a charming, solemn, elevated and piercing voice was his! Indrabhuti felt:

'Oh! Have I come to some other world? Or what is this? How splendid this samavasaran is! How have all these heavenly beings become the servants of the Lord? How his radiant form is beyond all comparison. How superhuman, sublime and incomparable his voice is! Only on hearing this voice the three kinds of afflictions disappear and we feel that all sorrows subside. We wish that we could go on listening to this voice. The doctrines expounded by this voice must be extraordinary. It is true that the world preceptor's infinite knowledge, incomparable form, sublime voice, his unique dignity and his excellent expositions of invaluable doctrines are beyond description. Therefore, when a worldly soul hears that voice how can he retain its ego? The poet says: "I have pondered over many subjects in my life but all in vain . Now meditate solely upon the word Arihant."

श्री अरिहंत पद ध्याईये चोत्रीश अतिशयवंता रे
पांत्रीश वाणी गुणे भर्या, बार गुणे गुणवंता रे

(Meditate upon the holy Arihant who possesses 34 transcendent qualities and who is the master of 35 merits of speech. "Even after attaining the Jineshvar Dev (Tirthankar) if we do not appreciate heartily his doctrines and if we do not have a deep yearning for the knowledge of true doctrines all our endeavours are futile".)

If even on seeing Jineshvar Dev one does not experience a feeling of approval and veneration and an intense desire to know the metaphysical truth, then all is futile. Indrabhuti did have this, therefore, the Lord tries to explain the Vedic statement thus. "You have understood the meaning of the Vedic statement thus: विज्ञानघन = consciousness; एतेभ्यो भूतेभ्यो एवंfrom among these five basic elements; समुत्थाय-emerged, disintegration of the elements, consciousness also is destroyed; न प्रेत्यसंज्ञा अस्तीति, this does not go elsewhere, it is destroyed. In the same Veda you get this contradicting statement स्वर्गकामोऽग्निहोत्रं जुहुयात्. Those who desire attainment to heaven must perform the sacrifice called *Agnihotra*. From this statement, you get the doubt: "If consciousness does not go anywhere, what is that entity which goes to heaven after performing *Agnihotra*? If nothing remains of this life, what can go to the other world? Is there any entity called *jīva* (soul)?"

The Excellent way of explaining the truth

What an excellent method this is of the supremely

compassionate Lord to explain the truth even to opponents in a convincing manner! First of all , he discloses the thoughts and doubts concealed in the heart of the opponent. In other words, he states them in clear terms. Even for this, he employs very affectionate words. This is an extraordinary method because it convinces even opponents of the truth. On account of this, the opponent becomes a friend and is interested with and by this method, his prejudices disappear and he begins to think of the right arguments. Otherwise, as long as he has his prejudices, he refuses to be carried away by the force of logical arguments.

In the great grantha entitled Sri Visheshavashyak Bhashya, Jinabhadragaṇi Kshamāshraman, the revered ocean of scriptural knowledge, describes fully and in detail Gaṇadharavad. The great grantha contains a clear account of the way in which Shri Mahāvīr Bhagavān by means of logical arguments cleared the doubts of eleven Gaṇadharas relating to such entities as *jīvas* and *Karmas* etc.

The arguments in support of the theory "jīva does not exist" and the arguments in support of the theory "jīva exists" are briefly propounded here:

The proof for the non-existence of soul.
Soul cannot be accepted without evidence:

Here the Lord states the arguments of those who do not believe in the existence of soul as an independent entity. We do not have the necessary evidence to prove that soul is different from '*Panch Bhutas*' i.e. the five basic elements like earth, water etc., and without evidence or proof we cannot believe in anything. Big debaters, controversies confront one another with logical arguments. If the evidence presented by anyone is proved to be unsound then the conclusion based upon that evidence and the subject of that evidence cannot be considered sound. There are many kinds of *Pramānas* (evidences) such as *Pratyaksha* (direct evidence through the senses), *Anumāna* (Inference), *Upamāna* (comparison), Arthāpatti (presumption), *Sambhava* (inclusion), Āgama (Scriptural testimony) etc. If we can prove that jīva (soul) is different from the five elements on the basis of any one of these evidences, then we can conclude logically that "jīva exists", but we cannot find such evidence:

The existence of *ātmā* (soul) cannot be proved by menas of *Pratyaksha pramāna*. To have perceptible evidence, we should be able to perceive it at least by one of our five senses, but none of our five senses can perceive the existence of soul. A soul is not visible like a pot. It cannot be heard with the ear like a sound. It cannot be tasted with the tongue. Thus, the existence of soul cannot be seen, smelt, tasted, heard or touched.

Question: If a *jīva* cannot be perceived by our senses, how can we believe in its existence? Though a *Paramanu* (atom) cannot be perceived with the senses, we can see its effect in the form of the pot. Therefore, we cannot negate its existence, whereas a soul cannot be perceived with the senses and the effect of the soul also cannot be seen in any form. When that is so, how can we believe in its existence?

Answer: In this world, though the soul may not be outwardly perceptible in the form of a substance, we can recognise its existence by means of Anumāna (inference). For instance, the fire burning inside a cottage may not be visible outwardly yet on the basis of the smoke emerging from its roof, we can infer the existence of fire in it. In this manner, we can infer the existence of soul on the basis of such evidence as the scriptures etc. You set forth a proof on the basis of inference, but, we cannot realise the existence of soul even on the basis of *Anumāna* (inference). Anumāna is of three kinds.

1. *Karana-Karya Ąnumāna* (Inference of effect from the cause): The feet of ants, the play of 'the ruddy goose in the dust storm etc, seen with dark dense clouds, are indicative of the imminence of rain. On the basis of these things, the farmer infers that rain (the effect) will fall; in the same manner, when we see rice mixed in water being boiled on a stove, we infer that food (of cooked rice) will be ready. When we see on a battlefield two hostile armies, we infer the possibility of a war and when we see the sun declining to the west, we infer that sun-set will take place soon.

2. *Karya-Karana-Anumāna* (infering the cause from the effect): For example smoke emerging from fire is the effect of fire. It is the effect from which we infer the cause which is the fire. The cause is the fire and the effect is the smoke. Seeing the smoke, that is, the effect, we infer the cause, that is, the

fire. Similarly, when we see a child (the effect) we infer the cause, namely, the father.

3. *'Samanyato-drishta Anumana'*: The first two kinds of inferences are based on a relation of succession. Now, *samanyato-drishta* (commonly seen together) is based on a relation of two things simultaneously present (coexistence). Each is connected with the other. In such a case, we infer the presence of one entity, on seeing a second entity. For instance, taste and smell or colour co-exist. In the case of a mango put into dry grass to be ripened, we infer in darkness also, by the sweet taste of it, that the mango has become ripe. In the same manner, the noise of the barking of dogs etc. makes us infer from a distance the existence of a village.

All these are inferences drawn on the basis of the connection between the ***Linga*** (sign) and the ***Lingi*** (the signified) or the ***Hetu*** (reason) and ***Sādhya***, (major term). What we infer from smoke is called the ***Hetu*** and the thing inferred e.g. fire is called the ***sādhya***. Whenever there is the Hetu, there must exist the Sadhya. The Hetu is said to be dependent; and the Sadhya is said to be that on which it depends. Between the two (Hetu and Sadhya) there is ***Vyāpti*** (the relation) of invariable concomitance. In the case of the fire and the smoke in the cottage, there should be a determined relationship (***Vyāpti***) between the ***Hetu*** and the ***Sādhya*** i.e. the smoke and the fire. The dependence (relation) of the two should have been known formerly. We have seen this ***Vyāpti*** or relationship in the kitchen. Therefore, when we see smoke emerging from a cottage we infer the existence of fire there.

Now, what is such a thing which is coexistent with a soul, on the basis of which we can infer its existence? As far as the *Atma* (soul) is concerned we do not have any such thing . It means, no one of these inferential basis (succession or coexistence) is seen because soul has no cause; no effect and no co-existential entity on the basis of which we can make inferences.

The existence of soul cannot be proved or inferred on the basis of *Upamāna* (comparison) and *Arthapatti* (presumption from an apparent inexplicability).

Upamāna implies knowing the unknown through the known which is similar to it. After having known a certain entity on the basis of *Upamāna*, if we happen to see it, we can easily recognise it. But we do not have any known things which can be compared to soul. Therefore, the evidence called *Upamāna* is not available to prove the existence of soul.

Arthapatti: If a certain entity seen and heard cannot occur without a certain other entity unseen and unheard, then the existence of the unseen and the unheard is established from the inexplicability of the seen and the heard. For instance, when we see a well-fed and well-grown person, and hear if somebody says that he does not at all eat food during day-time, it is clear that he must be eating food at night. But relating to the soul we do not find any such object which can be seen and heard but which, without the existence of soul, cannot be explained and on the basis of which we can presume the existence of soul.

Sambhava Pramāna (Inclusion): Even on the basis of *sambhava*, the existence of the soul cannot be proved. *Sambhava Pramāna* means inferring the existence of one thing contained within another thing. For instance, if we know that a person has one lakh rupees, then we can say for certain, that he has one thousand rupees. We say that an old man has seen youth because youth is a part of the long human life. But there is no such entity as comprises the soul, hence there is no such entity by looking at which we can assert that soul exists because that entity exists. We do not find such an entity.

Aitihiya Pramāna. (Historical proof): The historical evidence consists of such things as legends according to which for generations people believe, for example, that a ghost dwells in a certain ruined house. This kind of belief runs through generation on the basis of historical truth, but regarding the existence of soul no such legends or sayings are current, because no such legend about the dwelling of the soul in a body is current uptil now through generations.

Question: Among those who believe in the existence of soul there is a traditional belief that the soul dwells in the body, but is different from it. Why so?

Answer: This traditional belief cannot be treated as '*Pramāna* (Authority) since it is not prevalent among all people. Moreover, many legends and sayings which are current in a certain section of people are not an evidence; and can also be false and unauthentic. Therefore, on the basis of historical evidence, *Aitihiya Pramāna*, the existence of soul cannot be indisputably established.

The remaining ones are:

Āgama Pramāna and Shabda Pramāna (The evidence of scriptural words):

If the existence of a thing cannot be proved on the basis of any one of the *'Pramānas'* considered above, then we can establish the existence of even a thing on the basis of 'Agama Pramana'–'Shabda Pramana'. 'Agama means the words of an *'Aapta'*–person i.e. a trustworthy and truthful man. Just as a son can know on the basis of the words of his father that a certain person is his grand-father, so we can know from the science of astrology the time of such things as the lunar eclipse, the rising of the moon and the solar eclipse etc., Regarding these timings the fore-going evidences like *Pratyaksha* (direct perception), *Anumāna* (inference) etc., do not help us. Now, regarding soul, of course, we have enough testimony in the 'Shastras', i.e. Scriptures but the Shastras contain many mutually contradictory statements regarding soul. For instance, some say that soul is only one while others say that souls are infinite in number, whereas some believe that soul is momentary (i.e. transient) and perishing within a moment while others assert that it is eternal and imperishable. When such is the case which *shastra* should be trusted as the authority? And what sort of a soul can be proved?

So far we have tried to present the arguments in support of the theory that soul does not exist. Now, we shall consider the arguments in support of the theory that the soul exists as an independent entity.

The evidence in support of the view that the soul exists

The pratyaksha pramāna (perceptible proof) in support of the theory that the soul exists.

1. The Omniscient ones directly perceive the soul. Just as a particular man's inner doubts and reflections are directly perceived and visualized by him, who has such doubts, in the same manner, the soul is directly perceived, observed and visualized by those omniscients, which must be accepted and must be believed in.

2. Even by our direct perception the soul is really proved. The doubts, decisions, arguments, joys and sorrows which are directly perceived by us, are direct experiences of the soul itself since soul itself is these qualities incarnate, i.e. these qualities are not different from soul. Whereas the body is not these qualities incarnate.

3. "I am doing; I did; I will do; I am speaking; I spoke; I will speak" etc. In these experiences of the three phases of time, the experience of 'I' is the direct unobstructed self experienced by perception of the very soul, because in the present, the past, and the future the soul remains as it is, while the body goes on changing. It is not said; 'If I eat more I might be spoiled', but is said, 'If I eat more, my body might be spoiled'. Such is our experience. In this, 'I' means the soul and so its existence is established.

4. Who is the one that experiences a dream? It is the soul. In dense darkness, where you cannot see your body there the experience occurs as "I am" This unobstructed direct experience is that of the soul only, and not of the body.

5. When the body sometimes suddenly changes its colour or grows weak to a great extent, the doubt arises, 'Is this my body?' At any time, we do not get a doubt regarding 'I' even in that darkness. Such a doubt regarding 'I' never arises, "Am I existing or not"? The 'I' is always determined. This determination regarding 'I' is really the determination of the soul.

6. On the basis of the direct perception of a quality, the possesser of the quality also is styled as "Directly perceived". For instance, if the colour of a pot is seen through a hole of a curtain behind which the pot is placed, it is asserted that the pot is directly seen. In this manner by the direct perception of the soul as memory, curiosity understanding, desire, happiness etc., it is believed that the soul also is perceived directly, because the quality is not different from the possessor of the quality, rather the possessor of the quality is himself qualities incarnate.

Question: Are not the qualities like memory etc. the qualities of the body? What need is there to treat them as the qualities of the soul?

Answer: The body is gross an object of visual perception, inert. Its qualities are whiteness, blackness, weakness, fatness etc. but not memory etc. which are formless, colourless and shapeless as well as of the nature of consciousness. The sweetness of the water with which sugar has been mixed, lies not in the water but in the sugar i.e., sweetness does not belong to water but to sugar. In the same manner, knowledge, happiness etc. that are experienced in the body, do not belong to the body, but belong only to the soul. The relation of quality and possessor of quality can occur only between things of homogeneous nature. For instance, the quality of ash is not greasiness but dryness. In the same manner, the qualities like memory belong to the soul.

In this manner, the soul is partially perceptible. But the soul in its totality is perceived only by an omniscient person. He only can see it and if one likes to become omniscient, he must practise severe spiritual austerities. The ghee lying concealed in milk also can be extracted only by processes like converting milk into curds, churning it, by separating the butter from it and by heating the butter. Similarly for the direct perception of the soul we have to undergo spiritual austerities. In this manner the existence of the soul is proved by:

1) *The Sarvajña's Kevalajnan*– Omniscient's direct perception: (2) self-perception of doubts etc.: (3) the experience of one and the same entity "I" in the three phases of time; (4) the experience of "I" in the dream state. (5) the absence of doubt regarding the soul as "I" and (6) direct perception of the qualities of the soul.

The Anumāna Pramāna (inferential proof) of the existence of the soul:

Question: Doubt, deliberation, judgement etc. are inner experiences and they are the direct evidences of the existence of soul. If so, where is the need for using *Anumāna* or inference?

Answer: The nihilists negate all realities and assert that all our doubts, judgements etc. are illusory, unreal, false and non-existent. For refuting them, it is necessary to use *Anumāna* (inference) *Pramāna* to prove the existence of the soul. The inferences are:

1) In order to establish the truth that in one's body a different entity like the soul is residing, we have to use

Anumāna. Just as in our body, so in another's body also when we observe the activity or withdrawal from activity, we infer that there dwells in the body soul which causes bodily activity or withdrawal therefrom. Just as a cart moves because of the horse, so the body also acts, moves, speaks, etc. because of the soul in it. Moreover the body's activities can be withdrawn only owing to soul leaving the body after death, which means that when soul leaves the body, the body like a cart without a horse cannot have activity aimed at the attainments of a desired object nor withdrawal of activity at all from an undesired object.

Question: Just as a living snake can of its own accord contract itself, in the same manner, can the body of its own accord not be active or cease to be active ? Where is the need of soul in this matter?

Answer: Even a snake can contract when it is alive, not when it is dead. Even this example illustrates the truth that in it resides some entity which produces these effects. Whenever we like, we cast our eyes at something; we can stop seeing; we can reason and can stop reasoning, we can move our hands and legs; we can stop moving them. How can these capacities be styled as possessed by the body which is inanimate? It is the soul that causes activity or refrainment from activity.

Two sorts of vyapti

It has already been said that if we like to use inference, we should know previously the relationship of dependence between *'sadhya'* and *'hetu'* (major term and reason). Now it is necessary to state clearly that there are two kinds of *Vyapti-Sambandhas:* 1) the relationship of agreement in presence viz. *Anvaya–vyapti* (relationship through co-existence of two , 2) *vyatireka vyapti* (the relationship of agreement of the two in absence).

Anvayāvyapti (Agreement in presence): This is the statement of the presence of the *hetu* and *sadhya.* Where there is the *hetu* (reason) there is the *sādhya* (major); as in the case of smoke and fire.

Vyatireka–Vyāpti:- (Agreement in absence)— This is said to be present in a situation where the relationship is opposite to *Anvaya* e.g. where there is no *sādhya* there is no *hetu* as where there is no fire as in a lake, there can be no smoke. Another example, if other philosophers do not believe in the omniscient Jinendradeva as the reverend Supreme Lord, then there is no *Jainatva* (Jainhood) in them.

1. Where there is no *Anvyāvyapti* but where there is only *Vyatireka-Vyapti* we cannot make any inference, just as when we see a man doing strange abnormal actions, we infer that he is possessed by a ghost. But here when we have not seen a ghost, how can we find *Anvayāvyapti* e.g "Wherever there are abnormal actions, there is ghost's possession." We have not seen such a thing previously because a ghost is not a thing that can be seen. Yet where there is no possession by a ghost there is no abnormal action. This kind of *Vyatirekavyapti* is found, and if this is found, we infer possession by ghost. Absolutely in the same manner, activity and refrainment from activity are seen in a living body and not in a dead body; so, as in the case of possession by ghosts, we can make an inference about possession of the body by the soul. We can say: "Wherever there is no soul's contact, there are no independent activities".

2. A machine manifests a regular and particular kind of working, but the body as opposed to the machine manifests many strange activities. Therefore, we have to infer the existence of some entity dwelling inside the body as in the case of a body possessed by a ghost.

3. The body is like a beautiful mansion supported by two pillars; therefore there must be somebody as its creator and a governor of its actions just as in the case of a house or a cottage in a forest. The body is a machine-like system. All the activities in the body are mechanical. In the head there is the brain which functions like a highly sophisticated computer or a telegraphic office. It is the centre of such activities as receiving messages, communicating them, formation of concepts by associating meanings to perceptions by means of sensitive nerves and under that office there are for the enjoyment of soul the sense-organs, the eyes, the ears, the nose, the tongue and the skin which are media through which the sovereign soul is overwhelmed with joy on seeing the glories and gracefulness of creation. They are like five windows through which the soul perceives the world around by the intervening medium of the senses. The soul as the

proprietor-sovereign, by means of these five senses, enjoys such things as dreams, music, gardens, flowers, sweets and soft objects, that are presented to him. In the same manner, musical instruments are fitted in the throat of this mansion of the human body, the heart contains power, below it there is a store and a kitchen and still below urinal and latrine. Who has built this amazing factory? Who governs, controls and organises all these things? The answer has to be that it is the Soul. If we say that God is the creator of those things, he is proved to be an engineer with imperfect knowledge and abilities because he has created a body which is greedy of food and drinks and which has to move about carrying the burden of such foul things as urine and faeces. Why did God create such an imperfect body? See the pitiable condition of man. He can look ahead but cannot see what is lying and happening behind! Why did He create such an imperfect eye? In this world, some are beautiful; some are ugly: some are healthy and some are unhealthy; some possess eye-sight and some are blind. Why did He create such differences? If you say that all these things occur according to their *karmas* (luck) here the question arises "Whose *Karmas* are they?" If you say that they are the soul's *karmas* then the existence of the soul (*jīva*) is proved.

4. The body, the senses and the limbs are the objects of enjoyment. If so, who is the one who is the enjoyer? Just as there is somebody who takes delight in wearing fine dress, there is an entity which takes delight in possessing a beautiful body. Who is this entity enjoying pleasures? The two legs and two hands are like servants. Who makes use of them? The answer is that it is the soul or the sovereign *Atmavam* that extracts work from them. The *jiva* is like a sovereign king ruling over the body and residing in it. As long as the king lives in the palace, the palace is kept clean and all its parts also have a new look but if the king leaves the palace, it becomes desolate and ruined because without the householder the house is void and vacuum. If the gardener in the form of 'soul' (*jiva*) is not there, the body withers away like an uncared for garden. Who can take care of the body and can enjoy it if there is no soul?

5. The five senses are merely instruments. If that is so, who is the controller of the senses, whose purposes do they serve?

Naturally, it is the soul that gets them to do work. Pincers and forceps cannot work by themselves. Someone must be there who uses them and gets work done by them.

6. If the body, the senses and the limbs carry out their work in obedience to the orders of some independent governing entity, then who is that independent governing entity? The answer is clear. It is the soul. It itself moves the pupils of the eyes here and there to see as desired, and makes the hands and legs move according to its own desire. It can also, as desired, keep them still. The body cannot be considered the owner controlling these various activities, because it is a form of a combination of all those various senses and organs. The body is not an independent entity. We cannot consider even the mind as the ordering entity because even that is dependent. It does not like to drink bitter medicine; yet it has to drink such medicine. Who makes it drink such medicine? When a person is sick, the mind hankers after eating unwholesome food; still who restricts this mind and stops it from eating what it likes to eat? It is the soul that does this. The soul is an independent proprietor. The mind is the manager. The mind sends waves to the various senses according to the inner tastes, likes and dislikes of the lord and owner dwelling in the body; and impels the various senses and organs to engage themselves in violent or non-violent activities etc. Those who utilise rightly this very valuable independence in giving the mind a good direction, in impelling the senses and organs to be of the pure soul, in the right way, and who engage themselves in auspicious activities, can cross the ocean of *samsār*.

7. Who controls and regulates the various activities of the body, limbs and senses? Who checks the sneeze? Who makes the eyes close to stop seeing something undesirable? Who makes the feet stop in the middle, while walking? Who impels the organ, on seeing the danger, at once, to stop passing urine? In the same manner, who is the one that saves us from speaking reproaching words intended to be spoken due to anger. Who is the independent controller of such actions and activities? Who organizes all these activities? Naturally, we must admit that the soul does all these things.

8. When a quarrel arises among the senses, who functions as the judge to settle the dispute? As for example, the eyes

inform us that a certain article is made of silver, while the touch reveals that it is tin-coated. The entity that thinks about it and gives an undoubted judgement is the soul; not the hand or the mind; because they are merely instruments. When the eyes see a green mango they inform us that it is sour. But when soul makes the tongue taste it, and it gives a sweet taste it disproves the idea given by the eyes. Without the soul as the interpretor and judge, how can the dispute between the tongue and the eyes be compromised, since their objects are utterly different and individually independent and since their perceptions are contradictory? Who says, "By sight I find that the mango is sour and unripe; and by taste, I find that it is ripe and sweet?" Here we have to admit that the sayer 'I' is the soul.

9. This body like a house or money is an object of attachment. If so, who develops attachment for the body? The house, money, iron-safe, furniture and other such objects cannot exercise any attachment by themselves because they are inanimate. The one who develops attachment for all these is an independent, individual, animate entity. "My body is tired. Now it cannot walk around as ordered by you". Who says this? The body itself cannot say this. The one who has such attachment for the body is the soul. Now you see that attachment arises from practice, hence how can a new-born child have attachment for his own body? Since it is new born, it has no practice. Therefore, we have to believe that becaue it has attachment even from birth, it has inherited impressions of attachments from its previous births. Thus, the independent existence of soul as the link between the two births is proved.

10. Who experiences the joys and sorrows of the mind? A man eating delicious food is in a happy mood; but suddenly, if he receives a telegram which says that he has incurred a loss of thousands of rupees, he becomes sad on hearing this news. Who experiences mental agony? The joy of having eaten delicious food exists in the body; and no harm has been done otherwise; so, we have to believe that the soul experiences that agony. In the same manner, when we get a festering finger cut off, the body seems to have been freed from pain because it is saved from further festering and pain. But who worries throughout life by thinking "Alas! I have lost my

finger?" It is the soul which experiences this life-long sorrow.

11. The body of a child acquires its shape from its parents; still, at times the child is seen possessing different qualities and nature which are dissimilar to those of its parents. Why so? By nature, the mother may be irritable, while the child may be calm, cool and peaceful. Why So? It has to be admitted here that in the two bodies, there are two independent and different souls which have brought into this world, the different impressions of their experiences of their past (*janmas*) births. Therefore, the two persons differ from each other in nature and possess different qualities. The impressions or impact of both are different.

12. The potter knows that form soft clay, an excellent pot can be made, so he works on the soft clay to get desired pot. This signifies that for the activity or the withdrawal of an activity, we should have prior knowledge of the means of the desired ones and the hated ones. Then only can we move toward the means of the liked ones and withdraw from the means of the hated ones. A new born child has to suck its mother's breast for the satisfaction of its hunger. From where did the child get the knowledge that the sucking of the mother's breast is the means to satisfy its hunger. You may say that the mother makes him aware of it but that is not the case. She can place the tip of her breast in the mouth of the child. That is all. But who taught the child the process of sucking? The mouth of a child is not like a blotting-paper which can naturally suck the milk of its mother; nor is it a magnet which naturally attracts and absorbs milk. If this is so, why does the child give up sucking of its own accord, after it is satisfied? Consequently, we have to admit that the child engages itself in sucking because of the knowledge of the means and its desire. This knowledge that sucking breast-milk satisfies its desire is derived from the impact of the experience of its previous birth. We have to believe that the child's soul had experiences in its previous birth and those experiences created the impressions, otherwise who is the container (supporter) of the *Samskar* (past impressions)? The body of a newly born child is inert. So, it cannot be the container. What relation does it have with impressions of the previous body, since it did not exist in the previous birth? How can this inanimate body know what is liked and what is hated?

Knowledge is not a quality of the body. If the knowledge is not a quality of the body, then is it worthwhile that it should eat *Kheer*, a sweet milk-pudding first; and take curry afterwards and gather both in the stomach? The body has no consciousness. Are there separate compartments in the stomach? No, but there the soul is incapable of keeping them separate; therefore, it has to bear with all this. It is capable of placing them separately in the mouth and of chewing them separately. All this is the work not of the body, but of the conscious soul; and therefore when soul gives up the body, the activity of eating ceases, even if the body exists. This proves that the activity is of soul; not of the body.

13. In the same manner, in the twins born to the same parents, we find differences in respect of nature, fondness, habits, tastes, desires, attachments, etc. Why so? The parents are the same. In the same manner, one of the twins learns with a little teaching, while the other does not. Why so? One experiences great delight in carrying out religious and spiritual activities like worshipping God etc. while the other has less interest in them. Both grow up in the same environment but why this difference? It must be admitted here that those sufficiencies and deficiencies and inabilities arise on account of the varied impressions of previous births. This implies the existence of the soul.

14. In the lives of persons, we see the psychophysical activities of the mind, voice and the body; the desire for carrying out the four endeavours *(purushārthas), (Prana)* breathing, or consciousness of (jñāna-Darshan) knowledge and precept, the sentiments of anger, pride, deception, avarice, passions and the various *leshyas* (mental states) like the Krishna (Black) Leshya etc. the instincts, (*Samjñas*) relating to food, sensual pleasures, possessions and fear, the inauspicious tendencies like attachment, hatred, joy, lamentation, sorrow and agitation, perturbation etc. the auscipious tendencies like pardon, forbearance, tolerance, politeness, and non-violence, truth and self-discipline etc. Who is the possessor of all these qualities? The inanimate body cannot be the possessor of these qualities because though the body remains in the same condition, these tendencies keep on changing. Sometimes, man exercises direct perception, sometimes through inference; sometimes

he displays attachment and sometimes hatred. Sometimes he displays avarice in his business, and sometimes pacifies himself even on hearing the news of a sudden change in the market and he experiences mental peace. Who brings about all these changes in man? Not a single one of these feelings and attitudes is present in a dead-body. From this, it is more than evident that all these belong to the conscious soul and all these are the attributes of the soul, the effects of the soul.

15. There is need for the existence of some substance as the supporter of knowledge, happiness, sorrow and other qualities which must be congruous with them and should mingle with them. It is likely that this supporting substance is not outwardly visible. For instance, in wet ash, water is not outwardly visible but the wetness surely belongs to the water, and not to the ash, because ash is not a congruous substance with wetness. In the same manner the soul is not outwardly visible in the body, still the supporting substance with which knowledge, happiness, and other such qualities are congruous is the soul only. The congruous qualities of the inanimate body are its colour, shape, taste, fatness, heaviness etc.

16. In this world, doubt arises only with respect to a real and existent entity but not in respect of an unreal and non-existent entity like "*the-Sky-flowers*". Such a doubt does not arise whether in a small basket "*Sky-flowers*" lie or not. But we get the doubt whether the soul is existent in the body or not? Therefore, this proves the existence of the real substance like the soul.

17. Sometimes, an illusion or a wrong concept arises only regarding an existent reality. Because in this world if silver does exist, seeing from a distance, an article made of tin, the illusion or wrong notion arises that it is silver. In the same manner, because in the world there does exist an entity called the soul, the disbelievers of soul get the illusion of soul in the body that 'body itself is surely the soul'. In other words, anything that is doubted is real, existing in the world.

18. Even the adversaries can exist regarding an existing entity. If there are believers in soul, then only barbarians are styled as non-Aryans. In the same manner, only because such qualities as kindness, truth, honesty and righteousness are existent realities, their opposite like unkindness, falsehood and dishonesty, unrighteousness are said to be existing in the

world; their existence is assumed and implied. In the same manner only if a substance called soul exists, then wood, a dead body etc. are treated as non-living inanimate things.

19. Even negation is possible only regarding an existent reality. Of course, this reality may be existing elsewhere; and may not be present where it is negated. A certain gentleman Harilal, for instance, if he is anywhere alive, then only can it be stated that Harilal is not present in his house. When some entity like"*Dittha*" is not existent anywhere, we cannot say that "*Dittha*" is not present here. In the same manner, we can say, "The *jiva* is not present in the body", and "The *jiva* is not the body", only when the entity called *jiva* is existing in the world. The purport is this. Anything regarding which a doubt or an illusion or a negation or a refutation arises, must be an existent reality.

Question: Since Jainism negates the existence of a creator of the world, does not such a negation prove the existence of a creator of the world?

Answer: No, we have to realise what exactly is negated. The negation may relate to (1) *Samyog* (contact of two substances *(dravyas),* (2) *Samavay* (contact between the quality and the container), (3) *Samanya* (an entity commonly taken), and (4) *Vishesh* (an entity specially taken).

Here are examples of the negation of *Samyog* which means contact. (1) Devdatta is not at home. Here the contact named *Samyog* of Devdatta is negated in his house. This contact of Devdatta is an existent thing, so it can be negated in his house (2) 'Donkey-horn' does not exist but the horn exists so it can be negated. Here the presence of a horn is negated in a donkey; but the 'donkey's horn is not negated because negation of a non-existent object is not possible. (3) There is no other moon. This negation of the other moon relates to a moon similar to the existing moon. The existence of another moon like the present moon is negated. (4) There are no pot-size pearls. In this statement also, the negation is of a speciality regarding size of the pearls. The negation is not wholly of a pot-sized pearl but it is of pot-sizedness in a pearl and that quality of pot-sizedness may be present in other objects. So here the negation is not regarding God as the world creator but the negation is in respect of the world-creatorship in the *Vitrag* god which creatorship lies in causes like *Karmas,* etc.

Question: Well, if it is said that there is no god, then this negation itself proves the existence of God. Doesn't it?

Answer: Let it be so. By the name of *Ishwar*, the wealthy people of that name "Ishwar", or those who possess royal prosperity and splendour, and even the *Paramatma* who possesses supreme prosperity are proved to exist.

20. The word that is pure (not a compound word) and etymologically derived denotes a reality. For instance, the word, "*Ashwa*", which means a horse is derived from the world '*Ashu*', which means that which runs swiftly. In the same manner, the word '*Jiva*', denotes an entity that lives. One who is living is a *Jiva.* The *Atma* is that which moves through different modifications.

21. The entity which has other words and modifications is real and is independent by existence. The body is called by various names such as *Sharir, Kaya, Deha, Kalevar.* These various names of the body denote the existence of the body. Similarly, the words *Jiva* (the living being), *Chetana* (consciousness), *atma* (the soul), *Jnanawan* (the enlightened one) is the other independent word denoting the *Jiva.* Therefore they prove the existence of the soul or *Jivaraja.* Imaginary words do not indicate any existing reality; e.g. a peasant's Ta Ra Ra Ra faltering sounds do not have any similar other word. Such imaginary words do not denote any substantial and real object.

22. *The thing finally liked.* It often happens in life that we discard a thing which we like less to secure a thing which we like more. People discard their rest to carry out business, because they like business more than rest, but people discard also a harmful business if they can get more money by some other more beneficial source; because they love money. But a man possessing wealth spends it to secure medical aid for his sick son because he loves his son more than money. Since he loves his wife more than his son, if some grief is caused to his wife by his son or his daughter-in-law, he will advise his son and daughter-in-law to live separately. If a fire breaks out in his house, and if at that time, he is on the ground floor and if his wife is upstairs, and if there is fear of her being burnt to ashes within a second, will the husband go upstairs to save his

wife's life? No, he will simply jump out of his house because, although he loves his wife, he loves his own body more than his wife. There is a further step. If the daughter-in-law is tired of the tortures of her mother-in-law and finds the heartlessness of her mother-in-law, she burns her body and commits suicide. She sacrifices even her body. For whose sake? What is more loveable than the body? The answer is that it is the soul. The daughter-in-law thinks, "I can't bear this agony. Let me die (viz. sacrifice) my body in fire and let me by death go to the other world, so that I may not have to bear tortures". Who is this 'I' here? It is the soul. It is the soul which sacrifices the body to get rid of the endless agony and anguish.

23. The amity, regard and goodness shown by others are liked whereas quarrels, grief, agitation, the superiority complex of others are not liked. By whom? By the soul, not by the body. Here one that is actually pleased or displeased by these things, is not the body, but the soul, because the body does not gain or lose weight or beauty by seeing other's amity or agitation. It is the soul that experiences either elation or depression, either loss or gain, in terms of emotion. If somebody is laughing or smiling, seeing that physical gesture, we say, that this is a mere show. In fact, he is inwardly unhappy. How can we use the word inwardly, if there is only the body and no substance like soul? What do we mean by saying 'inwardly?' It means that the soul of that person is inwardly really unhappy, though outwardly he seems to be cheerful.

24. At times we come across some persons who remember a previous birth. Such things do happen. Such a person remembers that in his previous birth, he lived at a certain shop, house and children etc. These experiences are authenticated by the relatives. These things may be still existent. He may say "I was doing business here: I was living here etc". Who is this 'I' and 'my' and 'me' etc. You may say that the 'I' refers to that man's soul who has come here from that previous life and that soul remembers its past experiences. The body of the present life which is quite new has no contact with the body of the previous birth. The previous body is totally destroyed and the previous life is completely ended. Then who is here that remembers the past

events. It is soul that remembers, the soul being eternal and imperishable was living in the past life.

A SUMMARY

A brief classification of the inferences relating to the soul:

1. Activity and refraining from activity.
2. Entrance of a ghost: the possession of a body by a ghost.
3. The creator of the mansion in the form of human body.
4. The one who organises and controls the bodily functions and enjoys the experiences relating to the body.
5. The handling of the senses as instruments.
6. The one who directs the limbs, senses, tongue, utterances and the mind in proceeding or retreating.
7. The one who controls the movements of limbs.
8. The arbitrator of the dissensions (disputes) among the senses.
9. One who experiences that the body is "Mine" and functions likewise.
10. The qualities of children differing from those of their parents.
11. The one who knows and experiences the joys and sorrows.
12. The knowledge of liked and disliked things.
13. The difference between twin children regarding their tastes, likes and dislikes.
14. *Yoga*–(Activities of mind, body and voice); *Upayoga* (concentration of mind, consciousness of the soul); The psycho-physical activities and propriety, *Bhava* (mood): mental attitudes, tendencies and instincts like *'leshyas'*, (mental state) and *samajnas* (instincts).
15. The supporting basis of the qualities like knowledge.
16. Doubt. If the soul is doubted, it is real.
17. Illusion (wrong knowledge).
18. The opposite entity.

19. Negation. What is negated here, lies surely elsewhere.
20. The basically and etymologically derived uncombined world *'Jiva'*.
21. The alternative words, the other words.
22. The thing that is loved finally, that is most beloved.
23. Loved and hated.
24. The recollection (remembrance) of previous life (birth). What does soul mean? We must not forget that after we realize the existence of the soul, we must treat soul as more important and more loveable than our body and the perceptible world. We should be very willingly and strongly determined in our mind that:
    (i) 'I' means the eternal and the never-perishing soul:
    (ii) 'I' means the soul dependent on the *karmas* bound in the previous births:
    (iii) 'I' means the soul that is often untiringly committing on inauspicious activities of the mind, voice and body; and thereby gathering and heaping newer and newer burdens of *karmas* upon itself;
    (iv) 'I' means 'my' soul that is afflicted with and distressed by the diseases on account of the very body which is created, protected and nourished by the self.
    (v) 'I' means 'my' soul that will be dismissed at an unknown time on an untimely occasion:
    (vi) Soul that is wandering through the varied *yonis* (that is the place of being born in the *samsar*).

Don't Despair : Remember soul

We need not despair entertaining such thoughts as "'I' means not my body, but my soul that has been crushed by *karmas* from times immemorial. Then how can my efforts for emancipation be possible and fruitful? If the soul has been experiencing enormous afflictions and agitations through countless births as a slave to *karmas* where is the possibility of having an end to it?" Of course, we need not think thus in despair yet we must be aware of this fact so that we may not be enticed and indulge in the qualities of the body and senses and external objects, i.e., the enjoyments of sensual objects and sexual pleasures, carrying on incessantly their activities and propensities, which result in collecting terrible *karmas*.

What awareness is necessary? Don't forget the immortal soul:

We have to keep this awareness so that in the illusion of the pleasures of the mortal body, we may not forget our own loveable immortal soul. The body requires excellent inanimate objects, sensual pleasures, pride and prestige, food and drink, pomp and power, joys and jubilations etc. Ensnared in such enticements and cravings of the body, the soul commits sinful *Karmas* by committing such follies as developing an illusory faith, committing sins, devloping attachments and hatred, falling into the pits of pride and deception, and engaging itself in futile and sinful behaviour and sinful usage of utterances. Committing such sins the soul gets itself caught in the bondages of terrible *Karmas*.

What is body?: Where has the body to be caught in bondage? The body which will one day stop working, will break down all relations with the soul. The body staying in this world will dismiss the soul from her. In this respect it can be said that the body can assert its supremacy over the soul and paralyse it. It is now not at all prepared to have any connection with the soul and the welfare of soul. And the result is that the soul will have to be imprisoned in another body, in the next birth. And in that birth the soul will have to suffer inordinate agonies and anguishes on account of the effects of the sinful *Karmas* of previous births.

For the emancipation of the soul from all these *Karmas* and bodily enslavements, as well as births and deaths, even one's father or one's dear wife is not capable of freeing the soul from those agonies. Moreover the soul, for experiencing the fruits of such sinful *Karmas* has to assume an inferior state of a series of low births. There it cannot in the least engage itself in the sensibility, faith, and observance of religion, and cannot carry out elevating spiritual activities or austerities. In consequence living the life of solely sinful behaviour, the *Karmas* of a terrible nature increase, and consequently the soul will have to take birth in very many inferior and despicable states of existence and will have to experience countless agitations and agonies. Who has to experience all these things? 'You' have to experience them. That means, 'your' soul has to experience them. No one else. Who experiences the fruits of your *Karmas?* Not your body, but your soul, which has been and which will have to continue to wander through the confounding mazes of the *Samsār*.

What is the Meaning of 'I'

Yet you need not give way to despair or fear because your other form of soul is absolutely beautiful. On it you cast a glance and contemplate a little on that form of your soul. 'Your' means whose? Your soul's, whom you recognise as 'I'. Now you see the glory of 'I'.

(1) 'I' means the soul that achieves a victory over the body and the senses, by means of spiritual knowledge and activities of the devotion to God, and sacrifices and austerities.

(2) 'I' means the soul which possesses instead of false faith, the right faith, the right vision, the vows of renunciation and repugnance to sinful acts, hatred and disgust towards sensual objects and the spirit of renunciation, the quality of serenity, cheerfulness and the propensity to entertain sublime contemplations.

(3) 'I' means the soul that is capable of newer and newer sublime and noble contemplations irrespective of the condition of the body.

(4) 'I' means the soul which can bestow upon all the souls of the universe, the boon of non-violence and fearlessness and which embodies such lofty virtues as spiritual strength, ethical excellence, righteousness, celibacy and refrainment from sensual pleasures.

(5) 'I' means the soul that has the power of attaining an absolute victory over the inner enemies like attachment etc., and which can exercise such magnificent qualities as faith, politeness, discretion, indifference towards the world, refrainment from sins etc.

(6) 'I' means the soul that is the proprietor of supreme peace, poise, and serenity, supreme tolerance, supreme forbearance, noble thoughts, and supreme spiritual tranquillity etc.

(7) 'I' means the soul which has the potentialities of supreme virtues by means of which it can gradually rise up to the auspicious deliverance of the supreme state of soul's pure existence characterised by infinite and ineffable felicity, etc. It is not the body but the soul. Is not this form of the soul the very embodiment of beauty? It is the first in beauty and so it is the first in power. How can we become so fortunate as to possess such a beautiful form of soul? In this state of soul there is the occasion of being petty, caught in narrow conceptions and faulty propensities or actions. In this discussion there is no significant digression from the running contemplation and deliberation. Now we shall think upon the various 'Pramanas' (evidences) and beliefs and doctrines of various *Darshans* (philosophies) and testify the truth in them.

The Upamāna pramāna (the testimony of comparison) regarding *the existence of the soul:* We can establish the existence of soul by means of the Upamāna Pramāna because we have to employ the comparative method in this connection, and we can compare the soul to air etc. The soul is like air, just as physical indolence, inflation of the belly, a loud release of wind from it and such things prove the existence of air in the body. In the same manner, the various activities and refrainments prompted by the desirable and undesirable propensities of the mind, anger, pride, etc., which appear on the face, the circulation of the blood, the shaking of the sinews and nerves etc. prove the existence of the invisible incentive substance called 'soul' in the body. We cannot see the wind but when a paper or a piece of cloth is flying we say that the wind is causing it to fly or shake. In the same manner, we can say that the activities and commotions of the various senses and organs of the body and the activities and propensities of the mind etc., are all caused by soul, though we may not be able to see soul. Someone may say, "If the soul is like wind, (i) we should be able to experience its presence by the sense of touch, and (ii) it must exist in different forms in the various organs of the body, manifesting itself just like the wind called 'Prana Vayu', the 'Apana Vayu' the 'Udana Vayu' etc." Here we can only say that their opinion is wrong because an example can never be similar in all respects; it is only partially similar. Here we have to establish the existence of an invisible substance by means of a partial comparison.

The Arthapati Pramana (Deductive testimony)

Even by means of the *Arthapatti Pramāna*, we can establish the existence of soul. For example, Devadatta appears healthy with a sound and strong body, though he does not eat food for months during day times. We can deduce from this fact that he must be eating food at nights, because the robustness of physical health cannot exist without food. In the same manner, we can infer that the consciousness, the activities and the refraining movements which are not visible in the dead body, are seen in a living body, hence they are indicative of the existence of the soul inside the body, because without someone dwelling in the body and accomplishing these movements in the organs—voice, mind and senses, these cannot happen. Thus by means of the deductive method we can prove the existence of the soul.

The sambhava pramana (Probability evidence)

Even by means of the sambhava pramāna we can prove the existence of soul; because even the sambhava pramāna is a kind of inference. For instance, one hundred includes fifty and fifty. Therefore, if somebody has with him one hundred rupees, we can infer easily that he has with him fifty rupees as well. In the same manner, the tendencies of liking etc. and similar activities, the consciousness, and the movements of a newborn child indicate the existence of an invisible power and that is soul. The soul is one of these invisible things. So we can say by Sambhava pramāna that soul lies concealed in the body as the prime cause of all these activities and movements.

Aitihya Pramāna: By means of the Aitihya pramāna, we can prove the existence of soul. Aitihya Pramāna means historical proof. The wise learned people had the belief that soul exists. Even a layman may say, regarding a man lying on the death-bed is still alive, there soul exists in his body" etc. This is historical testimony.

The testimony of Agama (scriptures): The theories expounded in the various schools (systems) of philosophy

Now, let us think of the testimony given by the Agams (scriptures). There are six schools of *Darshanas* (systems of philosophy) namely Nyaya Darshana, Vaisheshika Darshana, Vedanta Darshana, Sankhya Darshana, Yoga Darshana. Let us also see what the scriptures of Jain Darshan say about this subject. A detailed discussion will be made further regarding the various philosophical scriptures and their beliefs in various types of the form of soul, and also a discussion on the point that two contrary darshanas expound two contrary views regarding this truth. But first we have to understand these theories in brief and then scrutinize them.

The Theory according to the Vedānta Darshana

According to the Vedānta philosophy soul is one named Param-Brahma'. The *jivātma* and the *paramātma* are one entity. This is monistic mysticism; but this theory is not convincing because among the *jivas* (souls) of the universe differentiations and diversities are found, e.g., some *jivas* are happy, some are unhappy; some are enlightened; some are ignorant; some are human beings and some are animals, birds etc., some are religious minded believing in soul, and some are nihilists; some are violent, and some full of mercy. In this manner, if there is one soul, one spiritual reality, in this universe, how could there be such differences and diversities? Moreover, according to the monistic mystical philosophy, the bondage and deliverance cannot happen in their true sense.

The Sānkhya and Yoga Philosophies

Sānkhya and Yoga Darshanas (philosophies) believe in infinite souls, but according to them sould named *'Purush'* is a steadfast substance unchangeable in the three phases of time, and hence not bearing charges of different knowledge, death, birth, bondage, deliverance etc., i.e. soul is void of knowledge etc. The qualities, the attributes, like knowledge, desire, endeavour, etc., seen in soul are not of soul but they are possessed by the substance named *'Prakriti'* (an aggregate of main three qualities named *Satva, Rajas, Tamas*. The 'Prakriti' is shining like a mirror in which soul is reflected, and the qualities and attributes of Prakriti are adopted as of soul, which is in fact an illusion originated by 'Avidyā'.

Now the questions arise,

i) If the soul is utterly void of knowledge etc., how can we believe soul as possessing consciouness?

ii) In soul what is the thing called conscience?

iii) If soul is not under bondage, what is the meaning of soul's salvation?

iv) Let 'Prakriti' be under bondage, but why and how should soul exercise efforts for salvation?

The Theory of the Nyāya and Vaisheshika Darshanas

These philosophies believe in infinite souls recognising the existence of the qualities like knowledge *(Jñana)* etc., in soul: of course not as the natural qualities of soul, but as the creative extraneous qualities (in being created) dependent on the causes and newly originating, when the contact of the senses, inference etc., are applied as the causes. When there is no cause, as in salvation, these qualities cannot exist there in soul. Now the quetions arise,

i) If knowledge *(jñana)* is not the nature of soul, then what exactly is the nature of soul in the absence of *jñana*?

ii) What is meant by consciousness, when the soul is devoid of qualities like *jñana*?

iii) In the state of mokṣa, according to them soul is devoid of *jñana*. In other words, if the salvation is utterly devoid of knowledge, will it not be an inanimate thing like a stone?

Moreover, the Nyāya Darshana (philosophy) etc. believe in the principal of 'ekāntavād' (i.e. absolutism) by adopting the *Ekānta* (absolute) point of view Nyāyadarshan says that soul is absolutely imperishable and absolutely Omnipresent i.e. pervading the whole cosmos. But if it is absolutely onmipresent and permanent and if it cannot undergo transformations the following questions arise:

Obstacles in the Theory of Soul's omnipresence

(i) How can there be souls in different states at different times?

(ii) Where is the need for accepting the path of salvation since it undergoes no changes?

(iii) How can it keep moving from *Janama* to *Janama* and from place to place, if it is omnipresent?

(iv) Why should soul experience and realise joy and sorrow only in the body but not everywhere, when it is omnipresent?

The Bauddha Darshan: According to the Bauddha Darshan, (Philosophy) soul is momentary and it is knowledge incarnate, since it is momentory it undergoes transformations, and the original form disappears. If that is so, the question is "who will have to experience the fruits of previous *Karmas*? If there is one who experiences the fruits of previous *karmas* he was not at all existing in the previous moment, then who performed those *Karmas*? How can there be remembrance? How can such gradual activities take place like knowing first and then desiring, and then acting? First, acquiring the knowledge of Tattvas, and then contemplation on them, and then deep meditation. These gradual activities take place in soul. But if soul is momentary how can those actions of gradual moments happen? If soul is wholly "Enlightenment incarnate", then it is only the quality, but not a *dravya*, or a substance. If that is so, what is the supporter of this quality? Who is the possessor of the quality? If you say, "It itself is the quality and is itself the substance", then what about the activity? Who is the performer of activity? In the same manner, how can other qualities be justified in soul if it is in the form of pure 'cognition' quality because quality cannot remain in any other quality.

Anekāntvād, Sāpekshavād (The theory of Relativity) conquers:

The irrefutable questions arising in various non-Jain darshanas are due to the principle of Ekāntvād (Absolutism). Looking from the 'Anekānt' point of view, one vital truth emerges from this discussion and that is that there are infinite number of souls in existence. Every soul, excepting those in salvation, is of the size of the body, being confined in the body. It is both immortal (permanent) and transient, meaning mortal. It is both the performer of *Karmas,* and the one who experiences their fruits of *Karmas.* It can be bound by *Karmas,* and it can also attain deliverance from *Karmas.* It is both knowledge incarnate itself, and a supporting substance also of knowledge; and it is different from, as well as in the form of, knowledge. The Jain Darshana which adopts the non-absolute but the relative (Anekānt) point of view, (the relative aspect, vision) believes the soul in all these mutually alternate forms. Owing to this, true scriptural evidence regarding form and nature of soul is available in Jain darshana. the proof of the existence of soul on the basis of *dayā* (mercy, kindness) *dān* (charity), *daman* (self restraint or restriction over senses).

In this manner, refuting the theory of nihilists viz. 'there is no substance like soul', (i) the existence of soul has been proved on the basis of the pratyaksha (direct perception), Anumāna (inference) and Āgams (the scriptural testimonies); and (ii) the nihilistic philosophy that soul does not exist has been repudiated and disproved. Here, Lord Mahāvīr said to Indrabhuti Gautam: "O Indrabhuti Gautam! If there is a substance like soul an independent reality, then only (i) such sacrifices as the *Agnihotra* etc., propounded in Vedas can be of a sound basis, and a heavenly state of existence etc., as their fruit, can be logically established as true. If soul does not exist at all, who would go to heaven after death? The body being burnt here, there remains none who can go to heaven. In the same manner what is the need of 'Da', 'Da', 'Da', viz Dayā, Dāna, Daman! Dayā (Mercy, kindness), Dāna (charity) Daman (self-restraint) are impossible in the absence of soul. The law of nature is "as you give, so you receive", "As you sow, so you reap". As you act you are to accomplish the fruit. Just as your soul does not like agony and anguish, other souls also do not like them. Then if you cause anguish to others, it will surely cause anguish to yourself, if not in ths life, surely in the next life you shall have to experience anguish. It is a valid doctrine that instead of causing anguish to others, you bestow mercy, kindness and benevolence upon others. Benevolence, magnanimity or charity is a duty of human beings because blessed are the benevolent. Our giving alms or exercising charity in this life brings a great benefit to us in the next life. In the same manner, we must exercise strict restraint upon our senses which impel the soul engrossed in villainous tendencies (in devilish propensities), and which bind soul with inauspicious *karmas,* which in the next life give wicked births like those of worms etc. Hence by keeping restraint over senses, these calamities are avoided. This means that if you restrain your sensual desires and cravings, you will not have to commit sins, in consequence of which you will be born in your next life at a higher state of existence; and higher births will give you virtues and bliss and there you will not be tortured with agonies as in the births of birds, animals, worms and insects, etc. or in hell. In this manner we can observe and practise the three sublime ethical principles implied in the upanishadic sounds 'Da-Da-Da'. This is possible only if a substance like soul exists in the world utterly different from the body as a different entity just like a body.

Now, the supreme Lord Mahāvīr further preaches thus "O Gautam Indrabhuti!

विज्ञानघन एव एतेभ्यो भूतेभ्यः समुत्थाय, तान्येवानु विनश्यति न प्रेत्यसंज्ञास्तीति ।"

(Vijnanghan eva etebhyuh bhutebhyuh sumutthaaya tanyevaanu-vinashyati na pretyasanjnaasteeti)

This statement from the Vedas has been thus wrongly interpreted by you. The word 'Eva which follows the word 'Vijnanghan', has been wrongly joined by you with the word 'Bhutebhyuh', instead of reading 'Eva' with 'Vijnanghana.' By reading that phrase with bhutebhyuh, you understand that soul is created out of 'Panch Bhuta' i.e. five basic elements.

You interpret the statement to mean that the soul arises from the five basic elements. But in the Vedic statement the word 'Eva' is to be read in its place where it is exactly put in the sentence and then this reading gives us the right meaning thus—

'Vijnanghana Eva' means that the soul itself is the embodiment of knowledge. 'Vijnan means a special kind of knowledge, which is a working consciousness that sprouts and flashes out that becomes only disclosed, but not newly originated. It means the soul possesses the inherent natural ability of knowledge. This kind of quality of knowlege constitutes the nature of soul. Therefore, it is a part and parcel of soul remaining non-different from soul, and therefore, soul assumes the form of knowledge. In other words, soul is an embodiment of knowledge. Hence, there happens the intimate contact of soul with the flashes of knowledge. By such true interpretation the soul is called vijnanghana.

The Anekānt Theory of the Quality Separate and Non-Separate from Substance

Knowledge which arises relating to such 'Bhutas' viz. the basic elements as the earth, water, air etc., knowledge which arises relating to a pot, a cloth, or water, is the knowledge that arises from the basic elements, but in fact that knowledge arises and remains inseparable in soul. Hence the implication is that the knowledge being inseparable from soul, new souls are created in accordance with the gradual creations of flashes of new gradual knowledge of pot, cloth etc. As for example, see that first the finger is straight, and afterwards if it is bent in other words if it assumes a curved form, this curvedness is not absolutely separate from the finger but it is also in the form of the finger i.e. inseparate from the finger. Thus the attributes like staraightness or curvedness are not independent substances, but are the form of independent substances like the finger etc. These forms are inseparable from the supporting substances. Therefore on being straightness or curvedness in the finger, it is said that the finger itself has become straight or has become curved. Here "*has become*" means "*has been created*". It implies that the finger has assumed a new form. In other words a new curved finger has been created, a new form creating a new finger. In the same manner, when we say new knowledge is created, it means that knowledge being inseparable from soul, and hence being a form of new knowledge has been created. From this it is evident that a new form of knowledge, by means of its relationship with the basc elements '*bhutas*', has been created from '*bhutas*'. Moreover, the knowledge being an inseparable form of soul on the creation of a new form of knowledge, a new soul '*vijnanghan*' has been created. The soul itself is changed in the varied forms of knowledges. This means new souls are created in accordance with the creation of new forms of knowledges, because the form of knowledge is not absolutely separate from soul. Inasmuch as it is also partially separate from soul, it is said that varied forms of knowledges "come and go" in soul, because soul is the container of the knowledges. Now as regards the creation of 'only Vijnan', when it is said 'only vijnanghan' is created, here by the word "only" is meant a negation of the other qualities of soul such as happiness etc. From this it is evident that the basic elements 'bhutas' impel only knowledge to occur in soul, but not happiness etc. to occur. 'Vijnanghan Eva Bhutebhyuh samutthaya' i.e. the soul acquires only a form of knowledge from its contact with the basic elements. 'Tanyevanuvinashyati i.e. on the destruction (i.e. separation) of those elements soul in that form is disturbed, that form of knowledge being destroyed.

When Indrabhuti Gautam was thus enlightened and when his doubts were thus cleared, he felt that he could not find such a sublime spiritual refuge anywhere else except such Omniscient Lord. Moreover he felt that to seek the refuge of others was in the end futile and fruitless. He also realised "since my soul also, in its original form is so faultless and perfect, my first duty is to safeguard my soul. So let me accept the refuge of Lord Mahāvīr." Thus being relieved of all his doubts, he with his 500 disciples accepted on the spot Charitra dharma at the hands of Bhagavān Mahāvīr. Renouncing worldly house holder's life he became an 'Anagar Sadhu' (asetic without any possessions of a house, an abode and wealth etc.)

2

THE SECOND GAṆADHARA: AGNIBHUTI

THE DOUBT REGARDING KARMA (DESTINY)

Now we begin the discussion with the arguments of the second Ganadhar. As soon as Agnibhuti heard the news that Indrabhuti had accepted Jain Charita Deekśa (initiation to the ascetic group) at the hands of Bhagavān Mahāvīr, he was shocked 'Ah! What has happened? My brother, who has never in his life known defeat in arguments, has surrendered himself for life to his opponent. Certainly, there should have occurred some deceit. Therefore, I must go there with an absolute intellectual awareness and vigilance, so that I may not fall prey to the snares of the opponent, and by silincing him and making him void of arguments through my incisive arguments I may release my brother from his snares." Thinking thus he, accompanied by his 500 disciples, proceeded to see Bhagavān Mahāvīr.

But alas! he should have known that not only his brother Indrabhuti, but even the great Indra, the supreme of gods possessing divine knowledge named *Avadhigyān* got enthralled and fascinated by Bhagavān Mahāvīr who had ascended to the top most post named Tirthankarpad and who was vitarag and omniscient: that he himself would be thus fascinated by the Lord: and that the Lord had appeared here only to destroy his internal enemy namely *Moha* or illusion. Agnibhuti arrived at the staircase of the *Samavasaran*. The Bhagavān addressed him also as he had addressed Indrabhuti and also disclosed the doubt of Agnibhuti thus: "Dear Agnibhuti you have a doubt whether such a thing as *karma* (destiny, fate) exists in the world or not? But you have not thoroughly and deeply understood and contemplated over the meaning of the Vedic statement."

Like his brother, Angibhuti also stood stratified on seeing and hearing the Bhagavān. On the disclosure of his inner doubt, he rightly thought, "He is an omniscient one! So, now let me understand the truth properly and fully from Him". He stood before the Bhagavān politely with folded hands.

The Bhagavān began to explain the truth to Agnibhuti in this way:

Why Doubt About The Existence of Karma

"Oh Agnibhuti . You are confused because you have found two contradictory Vedic statements. One of them is,—"पुरुषेवेदं हि ग्निं सर्व यद् भूतं यच्च भाव्यं" in other words, "whatever has happened (in the past), and is apt to happen (in the future), is 'Purush (soul) only". The other contradictory Vedic saying you found is,—स्वर्गकामोऽग्नि होत्रं जुहूयात्" 'In other words, "one desiring heavenly birth should perform the sacrifice named '*Agnihotra*".

You have understood the first one thus:"That which is logically probable to happen is the *Purusha* or soul only. In other words, all the phenomenon of the world occur only on account of the prowess and power of soul. There is no such thing as *Karma.* If such a thing as *Karma* existed in the world, then in the Vedic statement with the word *'Purush'* the word 'Eva' meaning 'only' would not have been joined. But here in Vedas say 'only the soul' and that negates the other things, such as *Karma* and time etc. That means soul is all in all."

But on the other hand, you have found the contrary statement: like 'Svargakaamo agnihotram juhuyat'. स्वर्गकामोऽग्निहोत्रं जुहूयात्।—(He who desires heavenly birth must perform the yajna, sacrifice called the *'Agnihotra'*. From this Vedic statement, you have understood that "according to the Vedas, he who desires to go to heaven must perform the Angihotra sacrifice. But even after the agnihotra sacrifice is performed soul continues in the same state of existence for a long time: and then after a lapse of some time soul goes to heaven. In that case, the cause Agnihotra is destroyed long before, the effect the heavenly birth to be created comes later on. Then how can it be called heavenly birth's cause. Without the medium of *karma,* Agnihotra being destroyed is not capable in the absence of inter-medium to create heaven. So there must be *karma* as a link between cause and effect. If without this link in the form of *karma,* the soul itself accompanied with the endeavour of Agnihotra would have been creating heaven, then just as the 'yajna' is completed the soul should have immediately attained heaven! So there must be a medium, a link, call it anything, but *Karma* is a link between the 'cause' like 'Agnihotra and the 'effect' like birth in heaven. The jiva attains heaven only on account of the ripening of this *Karma.* In this manner you have to interpret and understand the Vedic text. From this, it becomes proved and it is evident that *Karma* does exist.

"Oh Agnibhuti! You entertained the doubt whether in the world such a thing as *'Karma'* exists or not', because in Vedas you found contradictory statements regarding *Karma.* Moreover you are thinking of this in yet another way, and so you might be feeling that:

1) If *karmas* are not visible, how can they be believed in?

2) Even if they are believed in, *Karmas* are incongruent with existence. So how are *Karmas* (destiny, fate) believable?

3) Why can we not deny the existence of something that is invisible?

But Oh, Agnibhuti! two questions arise on this:-

(i) One is, can you say that a certain thing, just because it is invisible, does not exist at all?

(ii) The second thing is, can you say that (1) because a thing is invisible to you only, it is unbelievable or (2) because it is not visible to anybody, it is unbelievable?

(1) To answer the first question, you should mind well that there are many hindrances on account of which even existent things may not be visible. Yet we are compelled to believe in their existence. We cannot see our eye lids because of their extreme proximity, yet on that basis can we say that our eye-lids do not exist? There are many hindrances on account of which a thing although existing is not visible; (We shall consider them later:) yet we have to believe in it.

Be afraid of the invisible Karmas: We have also to ponder over these utterances of the Lord spoken to Agnibhuti. Just because we cannot see an object, can we deny its existence! In the modern age, we have such phenomena as electricity in wires, magnetic power in a magnet, and the capacity in the atoms, although they are invisible, yet people believe in their existence. But it is surprising that in the case of truths relating to Shastras or the religion or the religious doctrines or the philosophical principles, people say "Where is it seen? Is it visible? Show us if it is visible". Saying thus they disbelieve the existence of such things as religion and *Tattvas* and it is surprising that they do not accept them! By speaking thus they show their distrust in the scriptures, religion and philosophy. By neglecting or denying the existence of the invisible *Karmas,* they waste, pollute and ruin the lofty human birth which is of a very short period, a very short span of life that has been attained. They ruin human birth on account of their ignorance, on account of mean and irrelevant thoughts, and obstinate beliefs or fanaticism or for the sake of sensual pleasures that are transient. They court spiritual ruin , and in consequence, they create terrible agonies and anguish for countless lives. But they should realise that just because a certain thing is not visible or not understandable, it cannot be negated or disbelieved as something unreal. It must be understood that there are very many reasons due to which a thing may not be visible, or not known to us, but that is no ground for entertaining distrust in its existence.

Those who have belief in *karmas* and their efficacy, atleast experience this: (1) Very many things happen against their wishes; and (2) though they entertain a strong wish for something that thing is not accomplished according to their wish. Why so? Say due to *karmas* being not favourable. Then why should they not believe in the existence of *karmas?* Even if they disbelieve in *Karmas'* theory, they notice the gradual decrease in age and frustrations because of unfulfilled desires. When there is no change in such conditions in their lives then why not believe in *karma*-theory? Why should they not make their life blessed in this invaluable state of human-birth by believing in the writings of the scriptures written by the sages who were entertaining the fear of *Saṃsāra,* that means who were afraid of the down-fall in the series of births and deaths in *Saṃsāra* and who were the men of outstanding spiritual attainments and knowledge, living an extraordinary pious life of *saṃyam* (self restraint), and who were veracious i.e. who always spoke truth, and who possessed intensely unselfish and absolutely benevolent talent and behaviour?

Mind well this rarely obtainable and very precious human birth has been attained by us, for keeping complete trust in them. If the faith is preserved, further in future in accordance with this faith, the life will be rewarded by carrying out such *saṃyam* (self restraint) sacrifices, spiritual austerities, and keeping absolutely benevolent attitude, abhorrance towards sensual pleasures, and truthfulness and restraint over senses and mind. But if there is no faith at all, the life will go waste in sensual pleasures and enjoyments, such as eating, drinking, enjoying leisures, music, dance and so on. Here the soul lives the life of a beastly attitude. In the births of animals, birds and insects, these pleasures can be experienced by the flies, insects, birds, elephants, cuckoos, peacocks, donkeys, etc. Therefore we should value human birth and have faith in the words of the enlightened sages.

Things Though in front why Invisible ?

Now let us think over the reasons why certain things though they exist are not known.

(1) The things if very nearest to our eyes cannot be seen though they are in front of our eyes, just as we cannot see the collyrium applied to the eyes, and the movement of the eyelids.

(2) At a very distance, just as the telegraph poles along the railway track situated at a distance cannot be seen though they exist.

(3) Very subtle: just as such subtle object as the atoms or the radio-active particles (which are not visible if there is no beam of light emanating from the sun).

(4) In the same manner, if your mind does not concentrate on the idol, at the time of seeing the idol, you have no awareness whether the idol has a crown or not. Whether it had symmetrical eyes? Whether the saffron used was red or yellow. There are also many other reasons for our not being able to see the realities even though they exist.

What are the reasons that we do not see some objects though they exist there?

	The Reason	Things not seen
1.	Extreme proximity	The eyelids and the collyrium in the eyes.
2.	Great distance	The telegraph-poles on the sides of the railway track.
3.	Extremely minute	The dust particles visible only in a beam of light cannot be seen without it.

4.	The absence of mental concentration	One cannot say whether the idol had a crown or not when he was seeing the idol, because he was absent-minded.
5.	Impossible	One's own ears and head.
6.	The weakness of the senses	Inability to see letters etc. without spectacles.
7.	Mental dullness uncultivated or un-trained mind	Carats of gold: lustre of pearls.
8.	Being covered	A vailed (covered) object.
9.	Defeat, overthrow	Stars in sunlight.
10.	Nature	The sky, ghosts, etc.
11.	Being mixed with other similar things	A few grains mixed with a heap of green lentil and mustard.
12.	Mind diverted to another object	While concentrating on the taste, the colour is not seen.
13.	Forgetfulness	Something seen say some ten years ago.
14.	Loss of eyesight	A blind man cannot see anything.
15.	Wrong under-standing or perception	The gold ornaments (not of pure gold) worn by a wealthy villager or enforced upon a person by his deceitful friend, a goldsmith.
16.	False faith or 'Moha'–illusion	The realities like the jiva (soul)
17.	Old age or disease, three humours being corrupted	One cannot recognise things or persons in sickness though one might have seen them with familiarity many times previously.
18.	Without action or process	The butter in milk and curds.
19.	Mixed substance	Water in milk.
20.	Lack of training	Unable to distinguish a jewel from a glass.
21.	Devine illusion	Gold transformed into coal.

Therefore, we cannot say that *karmas* do not exist just because they are not seen.

(2) Now regarding the second question: "Because *karmas* are not visible to us they are not existent". We cannot

say this, because many things exist which though we may not see them yet they are in others' sight. Therefore, it is wrong to say that '*Karmas* do not exist because they cannot be seen by anyone'. The reason is, first of all, where have we seen all the *jivas* in the world so that we may know whether there is not one of them who has seen *karmas*? Even in visible *jivas* are we able to see knowledge – of what nature and to which extent? This we cannot see. Morever how can we say "In future too there will be none who can see *karmas*"? Therefore, it is not proper to disbelieve the existence of *karmas*.

Bhagavān Mahāvīr says to Agnibhutil 'you might have thought that there are "Three reasons for the existence of *karmas* being logically improbable:"

"The thing like *Karma* is improbable". Behind this statement are these three reasons:

(i) There is nothing like soul taking rebirth, and hence who can carry on *karmas* in the next life?

(ii) Let there be any one who may take a rebirth, but *karmas* are above rational comprehension. They cannot be brought within the scope of rational understanding, testing, and verification.

(iii) Or, it can be said that all things take place in this world because of the 'nature' of the things. Therefore where is the need for believing in *karmas*?

Refutation of these three reasons

(I-1) If there is nothing like one who goes to the next birth, then who will carry *karmas* with him? And for this life *karmas* are useless and inefficacious". We cannot say this because the soul taking another birth has been proved. It is for this reason that the Vedic statements like "they who desire to go to heaven, should perform the Agnihotra yajna etc." which you believe to be trueare logical and relevant. If the soul does not at all exist, who would go to heaven by performing the yajna?

(1-2) *Karmas* are beyond intellectual analysis, because here the question is of what nature will you believe *karmas*? 'Sanimittak' *karmas* i.e. produced from cause or 'Animittak', *karmas* those created without cause? (1) *'Animittak*: those created without any cause. (ii) *'Sanimittak*: produced by causes and reasons. Of these two points, (i) the first one cannot be believed in, because if *karmas* can arise naturally without a cause, then why is it that such 'Animittak' *karmas* are not produced in those who have attained Mokṣa (salvation)? Or why is it that *'Animittak' karmas* are not being produced always? If so, nobody can attain mokṣa at any time.

(ii) Regarding the second point, of *Sanimittak' karmas,* we shall have to think over the three causes by which *karmas* are produced.

The three causes that create Karmas

(1) *Karmas* arise from violence; or

(2) They arise from attachment and hatred; or

(3) They arise from other *karmas.*

Now thinking over these three, we shall see how each of them is not rational.

Why is it that those who with much cruelty slaughter a lot of animals and cut them to pieces with sharp implements, and also those who impel others to do so, are seen to enjoy happiness? They are bound by dangerous sins (inauspicious *karmas*) on account of their violent activities: then owing to their *karmas* they should be in great pain and anguish; but on the contrary they seem happy. As opposed to this, why are those who are always engaged in the worship of Tirthankar Parmātmā, penances and austerities etc. and who being merciful do not harm even the smallest creatures like ants, lead a life of poverty and adversity? Why so? Auspicious *karmas* created by worship, mercy, penances, non-violence etc. must bring happiness to them. Hence this doctrine that bad *karmas* are born out of violence, and good *karmas* are born out of worship, penances and mercy etc., is not appealing. Therefore the doctrine of *karmas* that they are created by violence does not remain logical. Hence it is not valid.

(ii) As regards the second point, if you say, "the *karma* is created by attachment and hatred," then the question is how do those attachments and hatred originate and from what source? If it is from *karmas* then we cannot say from present *karmas* they originate. If we say that they originate from the *karmas* of the previous life, *mokṣa* will have no scope, no meaning, because according to this theory, attachment and hatred arise from *karmas* and *karmas* arise from attachment and hatred. Consequently this endless cycle will continue further and further for infinity and mokṣa will never be attained. If mokṣa is never to happen then the shastras are meaningless.

(iii) As regards the third point, if you say that *karma* arises from *karma,* then this process coming down through generations, from times immemorial, will continue likewise in the future forever, and there can be no possibility of *mokṣa.*

Hence from the point of rationality, a thing like *karma* does not seem to exist.

"If there is no such thing as *karma,* the question arises as to how can strange particular effects and peculiar actions be created? One child is born with a golden spoon in his mouth, while another child cannot get even enough breast-milk from its mother. Why is this difference? We may say that it happens accidentally or by chance, without any cause. Instead of this chance if we believe in the *karmas,* we have to face conflicts of ideas.

A Refutation of the Theory that "Effects are created accidentally:"

In the theory that effects and activities arise accidentally, what does the word "accidentally" mean?

1. They arise without a cause;
2. They arise naturally;
3. They arise not on account of any external causes, but they arise automatically of their own accord. This is called *Swatma-hetu* (it being the cause itself);
4. Not on account of any cause but on account of some unreal substance (the effect is produced).

"Effect happens without a cause" this is a wrong statement, a wrong view We find everywhere that for an effect a cause has to be searched for, or obtained. It means if the cause is present, then only the effect comes into existence; for example if there is fire, then only there is smoke. It means, smoke can be obtained only from fire, curds is obtained only from milk, butter only from curds.

If everything happens by nature, e.g. the flame of fire goes vertically upwards only, the wind blows horizontally only, fire gives heat only and water gives coolness only, this is natural. The thorn is naturally sharp and pointed. If so, what is then the meaning of 'nature?'

The four meanings of nature:

Nature means own – 'Bhāva' (i) It may be the quality of an object; (ii) it may be the existence of an object; (iii) it may be the special object, or (iv) it may be its own nature, namely time-modification (modifications regarding various time-created substances.

1) Now 'natural' means they oiginate from the quality of the substance; but how can the quality exist without a substance that has never existed before its birth? And without the quality, how could that substance itself arise previously? If nature in the form of quality is deemed a different reality, then it is identical with *karma*. Is it not?

2) If we consider the existence only of a substance, as its nature, then what is this existence? Excepting the substance, nothing is to be brought from outside, as the existence.

The substance will be considered as the effect only and consequently, it means, its existence uptil now was not there at all. So how can it be worthwhile to say that the substance creates itself.

3) By the name of 'Nature' if you mean the special object, then here the question arises "what is this special object?" Is it a substance (*dravya*) or an attribute *(guṇa)* or the action of being produced? These three are impossible. If it is a separate object from these three, then it would mean the object is created from a different cause (but not from nature). Then how could it be called as created on account of its own nature?

4) If nature means time-modification of the substance and if a substance is born out of that nature, then how is it that the substances arising at the same time are dissimilar? How can there be dissimilarity in effects if there is no dissimilarity in causes?

Thus 'everything is created by nature' is a wrong statement.

Now,

3. Everything is *Self-Caused*: It is not sensible to say that something arises from its own self. Here two forms come before us: the own self is the cause-form and the substance is the effect form. If we say that something arises from its own self, then it is presumed for the creation of its own self, that original own self as the cause-form existed earlier. If the effect form is the same as the cause-form and the cause-form exists, then what remains for the effect-form to emerge? Which cause-form created the effect-form? Then it means that there is no such original form. How can a substance arise from its own self?

4. "Origin from an unreal source". This also is wrong. If in this world there is no substance at all like "unreal", then what is the meaning of creation from "unreal"? How can any thing originate from any unreal one? Such creation from unreal is something like an object arising from a donkey-horn which does not exist at all and which is unreal. Even if such an origin is accepted, where is the necessity for (i) someone to remain poor? (ii) someone to remain hungry? (iii) some to remain sick? Why should they suffer from poverty, hunger and disease? Because money, food, and health will then arise from the unreal. If the effects originate from an unreal cause, then their creations must also be similar but why should there be such dissimilar phases as childhood at one time, youth at another time? Or why is it not that similar-dissimilar things may appear simultaneously as cold and heat, health and disease, life and death?

It is, therefore, absolutely wrong to say that an effect arises accidentally (without a cause).

Three Ways for the origin of Karmas: Now we may see that ***karmas*** originate from (1) violence, (2) attachments and hatred, and (3) other ***karmas***. These three ways of the origin of ***karmas*** are logical and reasonable.

Punyānubandhi – pāpānubandhi karmas:

1. *Karmas* are of two kinds namely (i) ***punyānubandhi*** (ii) *pāpānubandhi*. The ***punyānubandhi karmas*** are those which when ripen manifest their fruit but at the same time create such conditions for the *jiva* concerned that would be for earning merits and *puṇya*. The ***pāpānubandhi karma*** is that which when ripens, impels the *jiva* concerned to develop sinful propensities. Among the *karmas* that we experience, some are auspicious, some are inauspicious. Thus there are four kinds of *karmas* namely:

1) *Punyānubandhi punya:* Auspicious *karmas* giving happiness accompained with virtues and pious mental attitude.

2) *Pāpānubandhi puṇya:* Happiness accompanied with vices and evil, inauspicious mental attitude.

3) *Punyānubandhi pāpa:* Inauspicious *karmas* giving sorrows accompanied with virtues and pious mental attitude.

4) *Pāpānubandhi pāpa:* Sorrows accompanied with vices, and evil inauspicious attitude.

Those persons who in spite of being violent, heartless, cruel and wicked in this life are at present happy are under the influence of the ripening of *Pāpānubandhi puṇya. 'Pāpānubandhi' punya* means the good luck mixed with sinfui impressions and propensities. *Karma*-binding is not created in this life and it does not ripen so quickly. Those *jivas* that earned *punya*, viz. good luck in their previous birth by means of charity, benevolence, self-restraint like celibacy, spiritual austerities, devotion and worshipping God etc. but who performed all these with the vicious aims of wordly pleasure and ambitions, enjoy wealth and happiness in this life on account of ripening of their good luck but on the other hand they also carry evil thoughts in their mind and remain engrossed in committing sinful actions like violence etc. on account of their previous vicious aims.

Those who performed religious ceremonies in the previous birth but with mean ambitions, sensual pleasures or with a view to take revenge etc., their wicked impressions continue in this life due to which illusory infatuation, attachments and sensual desires arise in this birth. On the contrary, those who have committed sins in the previous birth with disgust towards them and who repented their sins and at the same time performed pious religous actions, as the fruit of sins they have to experience sorrow in this life but at the same time on account of their previous repentance of sinful acts, they get opportunities to come in contact with *Sadhus* who are noble spiritual heads, and are also engaged in noble learning, noble thoughts and noble religious spiritual activities and austerities. They exercise the practice of virtues as also they acquire virtues. Thus they are earning *punyas* (good lucks) as their new spiritual wealth. This is the result of *punyānubandhi-Pāpakarma*, and on account of this the *jivas* experience sorrows on one hand and on the other they acquire such virtues as kindness, good conduct, spiritual activities, benevolence, nobility and devotion to and worshipping the lotus- like feet of *Paramātma*. All these good actions and virtues will bring them fruit in their next birth.

In normal wordly life, we find that those who eat sweetmeats etc. beyond the limit at functions or marriage ceremonies etc. fall ill the next day and will have to fast. When someone says about such a person on the day he is fasting that "he has not eaten anything today yet he is ill, why?", and if he makes the rule that "illness is caused by eating less", this rule would be wrong. In the same manner, if a person has excellent vigour and strength, if he eats something that causes illness or eats more than necessary and yet if he looks strong and healthy, here it will be wrong to make the rule "One becomes happy and healthy by eating too much food and sweetmeats etc." Because here health or disease is not the result of present activities of eating more or less but it is the result of such previous activity, whereas the present activity will produce their results in the future. In the same manner understand this, in respect of activities of even *dharma* and *adharma* as well as *punya* and *pāpa* (virtue and sin).

Therefore, there is no harm in saying that *karmas* (destinies) arise from violence etc.

Now let us think of the second point. *"Karma* arises from attachments and hatred". This theory contains atleast an element of truth that, attachments and hatred arise out of *karmas* of a previous birth.

Question: If this is so, then *karmas* when ripened will show their effect of attachment and hatred, which will generate new *karmas* and they too will create attachment and hatred. Thus this link will go on but will never end, there will be no scope for *Mokṣa*—salvation.

Answer: This is not always true that internal attachment and hatred always create *karmas;* otherwise none would have attained *mokṣa* uptil now. Infinite souls have attained *mokṣa.*

This fact proves that attachment and hatred being more and more controlled are one day wiped out for ever. From this, it is concluded that the *karmas* when ripened, although show their internal effect of attachment and hatred, but if externally their effects are suppressed namely no action of anger, no abusive language etc., then those *karmas* go fruitless. This shows that we can restrain our attachments and hatred and thereby frustrate the *karmas'* effect, i.e. if hatred arose towards somebody, by not spoiling facial appearance not using an abusive language, nor hurting, or injuring others, we can avoid the bondage of new *karmas*. For example, when we are angry with a person, or if we hate a person, if we restrain our passion and if we can avoid excitement, harsh words, and violence, we will not be gathering new *karmas*. A noble honest man may develop lust for wealth, but he may restrain his greed and may not commit theft or a dishonest activity. On the contrary, if he curses his own attachment, he can avoid heavy *karma*-bondages. We can put an end to this cycle of the continuance of *karmas* by studying great scriptures such as *'Samaraditya Kevali' Maharshi Charitra* and *Upamiti* etc., by understanding them, by developing philosophical and spiritual awareness and farsightedness and by restraining our attachments and hatred as far as possible.

The third point is *'Karmas* arise from previous *karmas?'* So long as the soul is burdened by the mass of previous *karmas,* it keeps gathering new *karmas.* Because, (a) if these *karmas* from the time of ripening give rise to vices like attachments, hatred and violent propensities, new *karmas* do arise.

(b) Even after we expel or discard these *karmas*, if our mind, body and voice given to us by *karmas*, continue their movements, then we gather new *karmas*.

(c) In the same manner, new *karmas* can not stick to the wholly independent, completely pure and formless soul, but to soul having bondages of previous *karmas* stick to the soul. These vices like violence, attachments and hatred are included in four causes for *karma*-bondages viz. false faith, vowlessness, passions, sentiment of anger etc., and sinful mental-vocal and physical activities. Now we shall examine the inferences regarding the existence of *karmas*.

The inferences regarding the existence of Karmas:

(1) The first part is this:-

'जो तुल्लसाहणाणं फले विसेसो न सो विणा हेउं'

If the other external causes and circumstances are similar, yet if two effects are diferent from each other, then it is concluded that other different internal causes must be working. Without such internal different causes, there cannot be such a difference in their effects. For instance two works written on different times by the same author dealing with same theme may mutually differ on account of the difference between the internal inspiration or attitude. In this manner for such differences as happiness and sorrow *karma* should be accepted as the inward cause. The difference should not be considered on account of outward causes such as delicious food, sandal paste, and woman etc., as well as thorns, cold, heat, poison, etc., which bring happiness or sorrow respectively, because on account of these very causes, some get sorrows instead of happiness, or happiness instead of sorrows. From this, it is evident that there is some deeper cause that regulates and brings about happiness and sorrows and that deeper cause is *karma*.

ii) If there is no linking *karman* body between the body of the previous birth and the body of the present birth, it means that between the two states there existed only the connecting pure soul. If so, owing to the pure soul how did the *jiva* attain a particular body in this *janma* (birth)?

Question: Is it not the result of the good and evil deeds of the previous birth?

Answer: No, it is so because a new body in the form of an effect arises in this birth and the good and evil deeds of the previous birth (which are the cause of present happiness and sorrow) have already been destroyed. The rule regarding the cause and effect is this. The cause must have existed in the previous moment of the effect. For example, suppose we ate food but suddently afterwards due to such an eatable taken by us, we vomitted the food, in this state why does not the body remain strong and healthy? Can the body grow strong just because food has been eaten? No. The body grows strong only if the food is preserved and assimilated in the body and transformed into blood etc. Here this has not happened because the food is vomitted. In the same manner, if we have gathered auspicious or inauspicious *karmas* on account of our good or evil deeds in the past life, these *karmas* accompany our soul to the present life, then only according to these *karmas* the present body of a particular form, shape etc. is being created. Thus the *karma*-body is proved in between the two births.

(iii) The *jiva* carries out such activities as charity, celibacy etc. What is the effect of these activities? Just as farming brings a harvest in the form of effect, benevolence, charity also must bring an effect and that is *karma* (destiny, fortune)

Question: Cultivation sometimes goes futile. Is that the case with benevolence? Does it also sometimes go futile?

Answer: It might go futile, if there is lack of other causes, but just as cultivation is carried out with this understanding that harvest is produced if the other necessary objects are present there, same is the case with charity.

Question: Can't we say that mental peace is the fruit? For instance, we get mental peace by giving alms to the deserving sages.

Answer: Yes. But even this is a mental activity. What is its fruit?

Question: Its fruit is other good activities like benevolence.

Answer: But what is the fruit of the last mental peace occurring at the end of the life which is not followed by any good deed of benevolence? In this case, it must be accepted that the fruit is *karma* or good fortune.

Question: Just as the visible fruit of violence is meat, similarly, the visible fruit of benevolence is praise, fame etc., but what is the need to believe in some invisible fruit? Normally in this world, people probably indulge in carrying out such actions as would bring an immediate visible benefit. You gave the example of cultivation. On that basis also, it must be accepted that there is a visible fruit of benevolence i.e. the capacity to show benevolence. When there is a visible fruit why should we think of an invisible fruit? The visible fruit of eating is satisfaction. The harvest is the visible fruit of cultivation. When that is so, what is the need to believe in some invisible fruit?

Answer: Every action may not bring about a visible fruit, yet it will surely bring about an invisible fruit. Therefore we must believe in the invisible fruits in addition to the visible fruits of our actions. Let the visible fruit of violence be meat but as its invisible fruit sin must be believed in. Otherwise why are the souls wandering in the *samsār* from the times immemorial? Because there are many who commit inauspicious activities such as violence, etc., many are the souls that are experiencing sorrows and wandering in the *Saṃsār.* On the contrary the number of those who carry out auspicious actions like charity etc., is small and so the number of *jivas* that get felicity and salvation is also small. Consequently good and evil actions are linked with happiness and sorrows respectively. Auspicious actions bring happiness and inauspicious actions bring sorrow, but this can happen only by the chain of *"kạrmas".*

Question: Many good actions like benevolence are carried out with the intention of attaining *"punya"* (good luck). Let them attain *punya* as the fruit of benevolence, but those who commit inauspicious actions like violence and other sins, they cherish inauspicious *karmas* as the fruit of sins. Then why should they get those fruits?

Answer: For the fruit, there is no rule of intention. In other words, intention is not always necessary for the emergence of the fruit. It is not always necessary that intention of the fruit must be present there as the cause. In farming if unknowingly some seeds remain scattered in a field, they do sprout and give a crop, even if no intention of their fruit was cherished. Therefore, the rule is only this that where there is a totality of the cause the effect will necessarily be created whether there is intention or not. It is evident from normal experience that the service rendered without ambition and expectation of any praise, prize etc., is considered of the hightest order and gives the highest fruit, and greatest benefit. Similarly here even though people may not have an intention for inauspicious *"karmas"*, violence and other vices necessarily bring those fruits. Why should we not believe in this truth?

If auspicious or inauspicious actions do not necessarily bring about any invisible effect, all souls would attain *"mokṣa"* at the end of this life. If there is no *karma* as the invisible effect of auspicious and inauspicious activities, how can there be after death any future strange state of *saṃsār* roaming in various births?

Question: Let there be the invisible fruit of auspicious activities like charity, benevolence etc., because they do not bear a visible fruit, but why should the inauspicious activites like violence etc., bear an invisible fruit, when they show the visible fruit like meat etc.?

Answer: You may compromise in your mind by thinking so and you may not believe in the invisible fruit of sinful actions, but then this difficulty arises that those who commit only sinful actions like violence will attain necessarily *"mokṣa"*. Those who do noble deeds will have to remain entangled in *saṃsār* to experience the invisible fruits of their actions, because then in the new birth (next life) also they will carry out such noble actions, due to which they will attain new auspicious *karmas* and they will bring again a new future birth. Thus they will remain entangled in the *saṃsār.* But this is merely a whim or imagination, because as a matter fact if all the sinful people would have attained *"mokṣa"*, how is it that there are in the world at present so many people who commit sins like violence, speaking false-hood etc.? If only benevolent people would have remained in the world, then there would have remained only happy people; but this is not the case in the world, because in this world countless unhappy beings are seen. On the other hand countless beings are seen committing sins. From this it is evident that the evil actions may have visible fruits, but their invisible fruit is surely produced and that is the *"karma"*. And those who commit such sins shall have to experience anguish as a result. In the world those who commit sins are infinite and those who suffer agonies are also infinite. It means that sorrows are the effects of evil actions according to mathematical equations.

Question: Those who commit such evil actions as violence do not intend to get the invisible fruit of their inauspicious *karmas,* yet they get it, and though we wish for a visible fruit of our auspicious actions many times, we do not get it. Why?

Answer: This also is a great proof of *karmas.* On account of *jiva's "Kaṣāya"* sentiments of pride, illusion, greed, anger and "yoga" bodily vocal and mental actions, the invisible effect namely *'karma'* is definitely created. Therefore, on account of actions like violence, the invisible *karmas* are definitely created. Whereas the visible fruits appear only on the ripening of the relative *karmas* of the previous birth but not otherwise. On account of this reason, though people equipped with the same sources carry on the same business, many of them do not get the profit they desire, or there occurs a difference in the profit they get. Though the visible sources may be the same there occurs a difference between the fruits of happiness and sorrow. Here it must be accepted that the reason behind this difference lies in the difference between the previous *karmas* which are invisible. Here you should not say, "How can a thing invisible work i.e. can produce anything!" because behind the visible effect like a pot, the invisible cause like atoms are undoubtedly accepted as working.

Question: All right. Then too, are not these invisible *karmas*, owing to their being relative of the formless soul, proved as formless quality of the soul?

Answer: No. There is no rule, that the substance connected with the soul always must be formless, because you see the body though connected with the soul is not formless.

"*Karma* has form." This can be proved on the following five grounds.

(1) The effects that possess a form have causes which possess a form, just as the atoms which are the cause of the pot, have a form. But when the effect is formless this rule does not apply to the case; for example, intelligence is a formless effect, but its cause namely the soul does not possess a form. Since the effect of *karmas* namely the body has a form, *karmas* also are proved to be possessing a form.

(2) Due to the contact of which happiness is experienced, that thing possesses a form. For example we feel happiness by eating food, and food has a form. In the same manner, contact of *karma* brings happiness, so it should be believed to possess a form.

(3) Due to the contact of which thing pain is felt, that thing also possesses a form. For example, by touching fire. In the same manner, owing to the contact of certain ripened *karmas* pain is experienced, so they *(karmas)* should be believed to have a form.

Question: Intelligence in the form of good and evil thoughts has its effect on our health. How can that principle be applied here because the intelligence is formless and physical health possesses a form.

Answer: Even there, the thoughts that cause those effects like pleasure or pain also possess a form they having been formed out of the *Manasa vargana* (mental particles) which possess a form.

4) "Those things that are different from the soul and from their qualities like knowledge and which are nourished by external causes, possess a form". For instance, just as a pot gets nourished and grows strong when it is treated with oil. In the same manner, *puṇya* (good fortune) is nourished by good deeds and misfortune is nourished by evil deeds. Therefore, the good fortune and misfortune have a form. In the above said words "different from knowledge, etc." are used only because the knowledge, even though nourished by external objects like the teacher, books and medicinal herbs possessing a form, is formless.

5) The effect of which cause is modifiable, that cause itself is modifiable. (Moreover, the thing *karma* is different from the soul, and is modifiable so it possesses a form.) For instance, the effect of milk is curds. If the effect curds is a modifiable thing because it undergoes further modifications like buttermilk, butter etc. then milk itself is a modifiable thing, and it is a substance possessing a form. The milk which produces these effects has a form and is a substance. In short that thing whose effect undergoes further modifications is itself a substance possessing a form and is capable to undergo modifications. In the same manner, the body etc. being the effects of *karmas,* and being modifiable substances the *karmas* themselves must be believed to be modifiable substance, undergoing modification. So it must be possessing a form.

Question: Karma is also the effect of the soul, and it is also a modifiable thing, so even the soul as a cause would be a substance undergoing modification. Is it so?

Answer: You should not say so, because *karma* is not the effect of the pure soul. But it is the effect of the soul bound by *karmas* of a previous life, and the previous *karmas* are no doubt possessing form and are modifiable. If so, the soul bound by such *karmas* is also in some respect possessing a form and a modifiable thing.

Question: For the strangeness of joys and sorrows, you believe in strange *karmas* as the cause, but why cannot joys and sorrows, rather than depending upon the cause, be believed as happening naturally like this strange modification in the sky, just as clouds, rainbows, and twilight etc.? Where is the need of believing in *karmas* to produce those effects?

Answer: The distortions of the sky are regular. The twilight occurs twice, once in the morning, and once in the evening. Clouds appear only in the rainy season. Even the rainbow occurs in the morning or in the evening when the sun-rays are refracted by watery-clouds. Thus these are mostly regular but joys and sorrows do not appear in such a regular manner. They appear to happen in an irregular manner. Therefore, they cannot be said to be happening naturally. Moreover, even the changes (modifications) in the sky take place at regular times and under definite circumstances. From this, it is evident that all these phenomena occur not merely naturally, but occur on account of some causes. In the same manner, joys and sorrows also do not appear naturally but they appear only when the creator-relative *karmas* are ripened.

Question: All right. Then can we believe that the distortions of *karmas* in the soul are also natural and causeless?

Answer: There can be no effect without a cause. Even nature *(svabhāva)* also is a necessary cause, but it must also be necessarily accompanied with the cause like time, endeavours, and instrumental means etc.

Question: Many strange changes (modifications) occur in the sky haphazardly without any cause. In the same manner, let the changes like sorrows and joys also occur in the body haphazardly, without cause. In other words, let the body itself be the cause for joys and sorrows. What is the need to bring *karmas* in between here?

Answer: The body is no doubt accepted as the cause, but note down this much that even the bulk of *karmas* is a kind of body called the "*karman* body". If you do not believe in this, how can the soul, after leaving the present body, and proceeding further to take birth in the next life, without creative (causative) *karmas* assume a visible and particular solid body? How can even that body be created of a particular type without the particular sort of the *karman*-body? In other words, it should not happen so. If this is so, in other words if there is no *karman* body to follow the soul after this life, the death here would bring an end to the soul's worldly relation and the soul would attain *mokṣa* (salvation). Another difficulty is this, if the soul without the body, relieved completely from this body has to experience *saṃsār,* then even for the souls that have attained *mokṣa,* the same thing would apply and they would have to experience *saṃsār* and so consequently none will have trust in *mokṣa*.

Question: How can there be a connection between *karmas* possessing a form and the formless soul?

Answer: (1) *Dharmastikāya* (the medium of motion) and the *adharmastikāya* (the medium of rest) though formless do come in connection with pudgals (inanimate substances) that possess a form. Only then i.e., they having connection can be helpful in motion and rest, without such a connection, how can this happen?

(2) This is our experience. The visible solid body also has been connected to the soul. Otherwise, how could there be any difference between a living body and a dead body?

In the same manner, the *karmas*, that have a form can come in contact with the soul. The soul in the *saṃsār* is not absolutely formless, but it is partly formless, because the soul, in past time during the infinite flow of *karmas* was in contact with *karmas*, like milk in contact with water; hence it is partly possessing form also. So, since it was bound (connected) with *karmas* of previous lives, now new *karmas*, which have form can be connected with such a soul which, being mixed with *karmas*, is partially possessing a form. That is why the soul which has been completely void of *karmas* and has attained *mokṣa* and now being absolutely formless cannot come at all in contact with *karmas*.

Question: Just as by the sandal wood paste or the stroke of a sword there is no beneficent or harmful effect on formless ākāsh (sky or space), similarly, how can good or evil *karmas* possessing form can have any good or evil effect on the formless soul?

Answer: (1) The illustration is dissimilar, because those things have no effect on the sky (space) whereas there is effect on the soul by *karmas* having relationship with it.

(2) By good or bad food etc. the effect, like benefit or harm on the soul, is evident.

(3) The intellect though being formless is affected in the form of benefit or harm by the herb nourishing intellect or by intoxicating drinks. Similarly, on the soul, *karmas* can produce their effects like benefit or harm.

Question: Why is it that *karmas* are the creator of the body etc.? Why is it that the pure soul (Brahma) or God (*Īśwar*) is not their creator?

Answer: (1) Just as the potter and the blacksmith can't create a pot etc., without tools, similarly, how can the pure soul or Īśwar create anything without proper tools? When the child is conceived in the womb there are no tools except *karmas*. *Karmas* are the only tools. Therefore, the creation of the body is carried out by the soul. If you say there are tools in the form of the union of the egg and the sperm, even that also can't take place without *karmas*, as the cause and creator; otherwise a body should be created of a pure and liberated soul.

(2) Without *karmas*, the pure soul or Īśwar can't be the creator, because it lacks the potentiality of action, movement. It is formless, bodyless, and it is either pervasive everywhere just like Ākāś or pervasive like an atom.

Question: Can Īśwar by his all pervasive body be the creator? Can he not?

Answer: If you believe in this theory that 'to create anything even "Īśwar" (God) requires a body', then the question arises, our body is also an effect, a creation. Now say what kind of body does 'Iśwar' possess to create such an all-pervasive body? If you say that this body is created naturally without the cause, then why should he not create the bodies of *jivas* etc., also in the same manner? If you say "yes, he does create it thus", then there arises the contradiction among the creations of varied effects only from the raw material without varied instrumental causes like *karmas*. Moreover the question is, what is the purpose of God behind such creations? If you say that 'he goes on creating such effects without any purpose', then can he not be called insane? Even if you believe for the time-being that he creates sometimes things thus without purpose, then this difficulty arises that then he should create all *jivas* alike, but why create *jivas* possessing strangeness and differences? You may say that he creates *jivas* because of compassions, then he must create all the creatures good and happy. Instead of that, why does he create some creatures evil and unhappy? If you say that he creates the creatures according to *karmas* of *jivas* then the '*karma*' thing is proved. Even then if you are bent upon believing in a creator-God you shall have to explain as also accept the following: The first is you shall have to accept God responsibile for the futile or controversial self-deceiving actions performed by ignorant and foolish men. You shall have to believe God's involvement in the actions like murder, wickedness, and the like executed by scoundrals. In this case where remains intelligence, gentlemanliness and benevolence in God? If God does not possess the capacity to prevent the crimes and faults of *jivas*, how can you style God as 'possessing all the capacities?' Moreover the question also arises that if he has no capacity to prevent crimes, then how can he possess the capacity to impart punishment? If you say that punishment is imparted by *karmas* of *jiva* himself, then this final conclusion is arrived at, that not God but *karmas* and *jiva* accompanied with *karmas* are proved as the creator.

Consequently the original question remains unsolved, "What about the Vedic statement '*purush ev idam gnim sarvam*' 'पुरुष एव इदम् ग्निं सर्वं'. In other words, "The soul alone is wholly and solely responsible for all creations, all which exists, all which is past, all which is to happen or which is governing the eternal, which increases by diet, which is shivering, which is standstill like mountains, which is at distance (like Meru), which is in proximity, which is in the middle, which is intermingled with all animate and inanimate substances and which is absolutely separate from all. This all is only the '*Purush*' (soul).

From this Vedic statement the existence of only the soul is established, but not of *karmas*. In the same manner from the Vedic statement 'विज्ञानघन एव' '*Vijnān Ghan eva*' also the aggregate of only *Vijñān* is established but not of *karma*.

But this is not a true interpretation because these Vedic statements are not meant to narrate the actual fact and figures but are meant only to appreciate the importance of the soul.

The question arises what is then the aim of such appreciation of the soul?

The answer is: The aim of such statement is to make one abandon the pride of higher Brahmini caste or higher *kṣatriya* caste and to create contemplation *(bhāvna)* of oneness with all. For example 'this man and I are one and the same in respect of the soul. Then what is the meaning of the pride of being of higher caste?

As regards the scriptures a discretion must be resorted to in the interpretation of sentences as to what type a particular sentence is. In normal circumstances some sentences are meant to inspire – to instigate power of good activity; or some sentences are for making fun of people, whereas some indicate the actual condition of the thing, even though the wording might be the same. We say to a student who is in despair, "you are vigilant and clever" and thereby convey that "you endeavour and will be successful". To a dull untalented student but one who pretends to be clever, we say "Brother, you are vigilant and clever". We say this to make fun of him. But when we say "you are vigilant and clever" to an intelligent and industrious student, we mean that he would easily pass the examination.

In this manner, we find three kinds of statements in the Vedas: (1) Vidhivākya (commands), (2) Artha-vād (praising or censuring), (3) Anuvād (explanation).

(1) *Vidhivād (Commands):* These statements command people to carry out certain duties and avoid certain other actions. For example, अग्निहोत्रं जुहूयात् स्वर्गकामः "He who desires heavenly life (birth) must carry out the Agnihotra yajna." 'मा हिंस्यात्' Do not commit violence.

(2) *Arthavād (Praise):* This kind of statement contains praise or censure. For instance, 'एकया पूर्णाहुत्या सर्वान् कामान् अपाप्नोति' All aspirations can be fulfilled by means of one complete bestowal (Poornāhuti). This is a praise of poornāhuti, but this is not a command to do something. Because if it were so, people would carry out only Poornāhuti and stop there only. Why should they carry out the Agnihotra etc. because thus they are proved useless. But by praising the poornāhuti, the text suggets that people must carry out atleast this austerity and that it should be done well.

An unconflicting interpretation of the Vedic statement. In this manner "एष वः प्रथमो यज्ञो योऽग्निष्टोमः" That means 'Agnishtoma sacrifice is your first duty', and here the text censures those who do not carry out that duty. The text suggests that people will have to be liable for going to hell if they carry out such sacrifice as the Ashwamedha and other likewise yajnas etc. without first carrying out the ritual called *Agnishtoma*. It is suggested so that people should take care of this point.

3) *Anuvād (Explanation):* Here is an example. "द्वादशा मासाः संवत्सरः" "Twelve months make a year." It is a statement of mere placing truth about a certain fact. Now in the running matter, "पुरुषेवेदं ग्निं सर्वं" This statement as explained earlier glorifies *Puruṣa* as all-pervasive; but it is not a statement to negate the existence of *karmas* or the nature of *karmas*; otherwise the Vedic statements which expound the existence of *karmas* "पुण्यं पुण्येन कर्मणा, पापः पापेन" would be wrong. Here are some examples:

An auspicious *karma* brings a good luck. A sinful *karma* brings bad luck etc. In this manner, as already stated without reference to the *karma* and by referring only to the *puruṣa*, the truth about a thing cannot match with a fact.

This explanation given by Bhagavān Mahāvīr convinced Agnibhuti Gautam and brought about a spiritual awakening in him; and he with his five hundred disciples renounced worldly relationships and accepted Sādhu *Dikṣā* at the feet of the Bhagavān. Agnibhuti Gautam got rid of his wrong knowledge and attained the right knowledge.

3

THE THIRD GAṆADHARA: VAYUBHUTI

IS THE BODY ITSELF THE SOUL?

On hearing that his two elder brothers Indrabhuti and Agnibhuti had become the disciples of the Bhagavān, the third brother Vayubhuti and other brahman scholars thought thus only "Bhagavān Mahāvīr is actually omniscient. When that is so, why should we entertain pride about our scholarship? We too should approach Bhagavān Mahāvīr and we too should venerate him and worship him. We too shall get rid of our sins by venerating the Bhagavān whom the three worlds glorify and whose refuge even such mighty scholars as Indrabhuti and Agnibhuti have sought. We too shall glorify the Lord and seek clarification regarding our doubts and the removal of them. So, the nine eminent scholars set off with their followers to meet the Lord. How full of faith they were and how deeply were they interested in *tattvas*. If the "two prominent leading scholars of our group have accepted the refuge of Bhagavān, let us also follow their footprints and do the "same". This was their faith. "If we can attain a life of the true *tattvas*, then let us give up this life of illusion". This was their deep interest in *tattvas*.

First of all, Vayubhuti accompanied by his five hundred disciples approached the Lord and stood before him. In those days, people had extraordinary love for spiritual education and scriptural studies and knowledge! Therefore, every tutor used to have hundreds of disciples gaining and realising scriptural studies under him. Every one of these eleven scholars had hundreds of disciples, carrying out scriptural studies and following them wherever they went leaving behind their houses and relatives. Those disciples were absolutely polite and intelligent possessing power of discrimination; that if the preceptor dedicated his life at the feet of a great man, they also used to follow them and dedicated their lives to that great man. It means that they always followed them in the real sense of the word. What is the essence of human life? What should be the pollen and the fragrant dust of the flower of human life? What is the noble behaviour of the lofty levels to which human beings should rise from the level of animals?

The cause for the doubt: Vayubhuti approached the Bhagavān. The Bhagavān as before addressed him by his name and *gotra* (lineage) and mentioned his doubt even before Vayubhuti said anything, "O Gautam Vayubhuti; Your doubt is whether this body itself is the soul or the soul is different from the body? This doubt arises from two different Vedic texts.

"You have understood one of these two Vedic texts e.g. 'विज्ञानघन एव' (Vijnanaghana eva) to mean that consciousness arises from the five basic elements namely the earth, the water, the fire, the air, and the sky; and that it gets destroyed when they are destroyed (dispersed). This implies that a thing like *chetna* or consciousness does exist, but it is the peculiar quality of the five material elements themselves, but not the peculiarity of the soul. It means that the body itself is the conscience soul.

On the other hand, you have obtained the other Vedic text, "न ट वै सशरीरस्य प्रियाप्रिययो रपहनिरस्तिं, अशरीरं वा वसन्तं प्रियापिये न स्पृशतः"

From this text, you have come to understand that there is no voidness of the joys and sorrows for the soul so long as it is confined in the body, and that joys and sorrows do not touch the soul which is entirely freed from the body and which has attained salvation. It is clear from this Vedic text that it propounds the existence of some independent entity styled as 'soul', which dwells of course in the body but which is completely different from the body, which soul governs and controls the body movements. On account of this contradiction between two Vedic texts, the doubt arose naturally.

The theory that – the body, an aggregation (collection, combination) of the basic elements, is itself the soul' – is supported by this outward illustration of liquor. It is prepared out of flowers of a kind of grass, jaggery and water. None of these ingredients of liquor individually possess intoxicating power, but it appears when they are combined. From this it is evident that the intoxicating power does not lie in any of these substances individually, and it arises from their combination; and that this intoxicating power is not a different entity but is a peculiarity, dharma or nature of the aggregation of three ingredients. Similarly conscience and conscienceness is the *dharma* of the aggregation of the basic five elements, but is not an independent and different entity. Thus it is argued that the soul or consciousness is merely the *dharma* of the aggregation of the basic elements but not a different entity.

The Argument Regarding the Theory "The Soul is Different from the body".

1) It is necessary to realise this vital truth. "How can something which is not the nature of each of the substances, be the nature of the aggregation of those substances?" We know that there is no oil in a sand particle. If we grind millions of sand particles, can we get even a drop of oil? Since in each grain of sesame there is oil, however little the quantity be, we get oil when we grind a large quantity of sesame grains. In the same manner, in liquor also since the effect of intoxication sweetness and coolness that are experienced, are present atleast to a little extent in grass, flowers, jaggery and water, respectively its clear experience is manifested in the aggregate of these substances when mixed and combined with each other. Otherwise, people could have prepared liquor by mixing (combining) any other substances. Therefore the inference is that what is present in each substance manifests itself in the aggregation in a higher degree.

Question: Then shall we believe that there is *chetan* or consciousness in every *bhuta* (basic element)? If so, why does not consciousness appear in every *bhuta* (basic element)? You can say 'it is latent, therefore it is not visible, and when the five elements combine, it becomes visible'.

Answer: It means, "when the element *(bhuta)* is single, there is no other veil on the *chetan* or consciousness to envelop it; in other words the element itself is in the form of a veil, on account of which, the *chetan* or the consciousness is not visible, and when combined with other *bhutas* (elements), the same each element in aggregation becomes the revealer of the latent consciousness lying in it". But this is a contradiction. Can a veil become the revealer of a reality?

Question: No. It is not so. The element that is not combined with other elements is a veil, and the elements when aggregated possess a special type of combination on account of which they manifest *chetan* (meaning consciousness). Each element has no consciousness separately, but in combination it has; hence it is manifested in the combination. You may say that if it is present in combination it must be present in the individual. Let it be so, but it is not visible because the element is itself the cover (veil).

Answer: This kind of special combination of elements is present even in a dead body, but there is no consciousness visible in it. Why is it so? What is the cause for it? If the absence of wind or warmth is the cause, those things can be supplied to the dead body.

Question: No. How can you produce the various kinds of winds like *'Prān'* and *'Udān'* etc. These things are not present in a dead body. Therefore there is no consciousness in it.

Answer: It means "you establish the winds such as Prān and Udān as the regulator of consciousness and knowledge, whereas the true position is different from this. Consciousness *chetan* itself is the regulator of the winds called Prān etc. We see that those who perform Prāṇāyām (breathing exercise) inhale and exhale wind in accordance with their volition (choice, desire). The essential point is that there is no consciousness in a dead body; therefore it implies that consciousness is not a natural quality of the *bhutas* or elements.

Question: Then, let us say that consciousness originates from the consciousness of the mother and it exists in the body until death. Now, what harm is there in this?

Answer: The harm is this. There is this great difficulty in believing so. Why is it that the *saṃskāras* (the innate impressions) of the mother's consciousness are not inherited by the child? If the mother is by nature irritable, the son may be by nature calm or vice versa. What is the cause behind this difference? If you say that some inherited characteristics are attained by the children, the question is why are they not present in the lice which originates from the same mother? If it is said that consciousness arises from the combination of the semen and menses, how did the lice without that combination get that consciousness even though it may be very small, or short lived? If you say,"the mother causes the emergence of the consciousness in the child that continues till death", then the question arises what is death? If you say that it is the destruction of consciousness, then its implication is that "the consciousness is created as such that it exists until it gets destroyed"; but the question is what is the cause for the destruction of consciousness? It will not be correct to say that it is caused by disproportion, unevenness in the three humours of airbilious fluid and cough," because when this unevenness disappears after death, the maladies like fever and bronchitis (cough) caused by the disproportion of the humours do not appear. Therefore, it has to be believed that the disproportion has disappeared and air–bilious fluid and cough have been changed from disproportionate to proportionate amount; and it is said in the medical scriptures "तेषां समत्वमारोग्ये" "In other words their evenness is conducive to health, then he has to be alive again. You yourself say that *chaitanya* or consciousness exists when the humours are in the right proportion.

Question: There is no proportionate humour at all because there pollution of blood etc., in the aberrations are not abolished. When that is so, how can consciousness appear again?

Answer: Then the question is why are not the pollutions abolished? Were they curable or not? If they were curable then they must be cured by means of medical treatment. If they were not curable, why were they incurable? Were they incurable because of (1) the absence of doctors or (2) the absence of medicines or (3) the ending of the span of life?

(1) It cannot be on account of the absence of doctors, because though there are doctors to treat them, many die.

(2) In the same manner, it cannot also be on account of the absence of medicines, the same medicines brought about a cure in the past.

(3) If you say that it is because of the ending of the span of life, viz, *āyushya karma*, then the question is where did this *āyushya karma* emerge and why is there the difference of time in the deaths of two sons of the same mother? Here is another proof to show that *āyushya karma* cannot be *dharma* or *nature* of the body embodying *chaitanya* or consciousness; otherwise, so long as the body exists that *āyushya-karma*

would not have been destroyed. So you must accept that the soul itself has brought with it such *karma* viz. *'āyushya-karma'* from previous birth, on the ending of which the relationship of the soul with the present body ended; hence, there appears no consciousness in the dead body. The essence of this argument is that *chaitanya* or consciousness is not at all the nature of the body. You might say *"Chaitanya* though being the nature of *bhutas*, on death, there is no special contact in five *bhuta*-particles of a dead body, or the special contact has left the body, hence there is no *chaitanya* (i.e., consciousness) in the dead body". If you say so, the meaning of "Special contact has left the body" is that 'the soul has left the body'.

Question: If you say that "*chaitanya* or consciousness is not the nature of the body and that it is of a different object", it is like saying that "a pot's redness does not belong to the pot, but it is of a different object". Does not this kind of belief seem a contradiction of the true concrete reality? Does it not seem quite contrary to the visible? (Contrary to the *pratyaksha.*)

Answer: What is the use of believing in only *pratyaksha* evidence? The sprout that comes from the earth seems to be of the earth, but it is not of the earth. Can it be believed to be the nature of the earth even to a little extent? Not at all. It is the nature of the seed. Otherwise, without the seed why is it not seen coming out of the earth? Hence, it shows that a sprout is the nature of the seed, but not of the earth.

(1) In the same manner, since in the absence of the soul, there is no consciousness seen in any body, we must believe that the nature of consciousness belongs not to the body but to the soul. Where we find an *Anumāna* (inference) that contradicts the *Pratyaksha*, the visible contradiction becomes negligible. Suppose a man has not eaten food today since morning and in the afternoon he experiences stomach-ache; this stomach-ache is not caused by his remaining hungry today but the ache has occurred due to the excessive quantity of food eaten on the previous day. Where we get an inference (*anumāna prāmāna*) of the existence of the soul, it makes the *'pratyaksha-virodh'*, viz., the contradiction of the 'visible' evidence negligible).

Evidences : Soul is different from Senses:

(2) Now these are the evidences of the existence of the soul as different from the senses:

That which even after the ending of the activities of senses, can retain the capacity for memory is different from them. For instance, after seeing through the five windows of a house, even after the windows are closed, the man can remember what he has seen, and he is different from the windows. Just as the person is seer, but the windows are not seers, so also the soul is the seer and senses are not seers; because:

(3) Sometimes even though the senses themselves are engaged in the activity towards a particular object, if the mind is elsewhere or has become blank, that object is not perceived. This implies that the senses are not seers.

(4) Even after the activiites of the senses have ceased, the person experienced has memory of perceived things. This means that the seer was not the senses but the soul of that person.

(5) Even after perceiving through the senses, one who experiences remembrance or carries out such sensations as contemplations, aberration, anxiety, or rejection etc., is someone else residing within the body.

From this, it is evident that the senses which are made of basic elments, '*bhutas*' are not the soul but are merely windows, and that the soul is a separate entity different from the senses, and he makes use of all these means, these instrumental objects like senses.

(6) For instance, just as someone looks out through a window and sees some person, and calls him through another window. These two windows do not have the power of unification of conceptual experience. Therefore, the one that unifies these conceptual experience of two windows is different from the windows. In the same manner, when one sees somebody eating a raw and sour mango, his tongue waters or his teeth grow sour. In such a case the one that experiences these two mixed sense-responses, these two combined sensations must be different from them, (viz. the senses), and must be of one soul.

(7) For instance out of five people each may have knowledge of five different objects but each knowing a separate object, what one knows, the other may not know.

There is the sixth one who has the knowledge of all these five objects; then this sixth one is different from all the five. In the same manner, the soul that remembers the experience of all the five objects perceived by all these five senses must be a different entity from them. The senses of their own accord cannot do anything. Knowledge arises only by the interaction of the mind with the soul. Here a question may arise: "Does the senses have the quality of knowledge?"

(8) (9) (10) (11) It is a rule that knowledge is preceded by knowledge. According to this rule the first knowledge occurring in this body should have been preceded by knowledge. Who is the possessor of this previous knowledge? Say, it is the soul. Similarly, it is in desire, it is in the body. A desire is always preceded by desire. A body is always preceded by fear and anguish. The inference is 'any desire, body, passions, sorrows and joys are preceded by desire, body, sorrows and joys'. The entity that experiences those preceding desire etc., is the soul itself.

(12) Like the relationship between the seed and sprout, the chain of relationships between body and *karma* has been flowing like a flood from times immemorial. This cannot go on without the creator i.e. *'karta'* the doer (the soul that is different from the body).

(13) When a pot is made with the help of a wooden stick, the stick is not the doer; it is only an instrument. In the same manner, the body itself is not the doer of the activities of the body. It is only an instrument, a means. Just as the potter is the doer in the case of a pot, here the doer of bodily activities is the soul.

(14) to (18) As it is said in the section relating to the first Ganadhar (i) Just as a house, similarly the body must have its creator which has a particular shape, or doer who is different from the body. (ii) Just as we wash and clean our dirty clothes and dye them and feel pleased with them, there is one who washes and cleans the body and beautifies it to make it beautiful and splendid: moreover enjoys and develops attachment for it and experiences those pleasures is not the body itself. The experiencer must be a separate entity different from the body. (Here for that entity the body is like a dress). (iii) Who is that which loves and desires the safety of the hands, the legs, the head etc. like the safety of pillars,

windows, doors of the house? The lover of the safety is not the body, because the body like a house is merely an aggregation, a combination of limbs and organs like parts of a building. (iv) Just as there is a relationship of the receiver and the received between metal and forceps, there is a similar relationship between the senses and their objects. This relationship between the senses and objects is that of a capturer and captured. For the existence of this kind of relationship between the senses and the sensual objects there is the need of a soul, comparable to a blacksmith, who has a volition of his own for capturing objects and knowing them. (v) That entity which can remember the experiences of another place and another time is imperishable. In the same manner, this is one argument that because one cannot remember the experiences of another, even though the body of the previous birth perishes, still that entity called soul that can remember those experiences in the new body, viz., bodily existence is surely different from the body.

The Theory of Momentary existence is not proper, how?

Question: Can we not remember the past experiences due to the impressions continued in the series of previous moments? We can remember. When that is so, where is the need for an imperishable soul of non-momentary existence?

Answer: Even in the momentary tradition of existence, there is the need for an individual who is interwoven in the series of moments and who is blessed and is imbued with memories and who retains impression of knowledge and experiences. Otherwise, after knowledge and experience perish, there cannot occur remembrances similar to them.

(19) Without one individual who has visualized all the things of the world as momentary who can say whichever is existent is momentary? Such a sayer passing through the series of all moments must be himself imperishable. Otherwise how can he himself if momentary, know that 'Things are momentary?' Without visualizing them as to their momentary natures, it is impossible for him to say so. In the same manner, if one himself existing momentarily perishes afterwards, then since he has no connection, no contact, no relationship with the past or the future, how can he know what happened in the past and what will happen in the future?

The point is that there is the need for an imperishable soul who sees and knows the whole series of the past and future.

Question: "All are like us" means "all being existent like us are momentary". In this manner, can't we know all as momentary in their existence?

Answer: Even to know this, first we must know and realise and visualize the realness in all. As the realness is visualized, as present in us so realness must be visualized as present in all worldly things. Then only can we say emphatically that all real things are momentary. If there is no capacity in us to know all the real things, how can we deduce that whatever is real is momentary?

Otherwise even an unreal thing will be proved to be momentary, (meaning perishable in a moment). Here you can't say 'oh, let it be so', because 'momentary' means that which stays, exists only one moment and is destroyed in the next moment. Now when an unreal thing does not exist at all, how can it be called existing (staying) one moment and perishing in the next moment? It means, destruction happens only of a real thing.

Now you see, no one can propound this theory that 'In the world all the real things are momentary'. First, because when he has no knowledge of all the past, present and future things, how can he establish a truth pertaining to all? Secondly, because when the propounder himself being momentary perishes in the next moment even before he is in a position to realise the momentariness of anything, how can he propound that theory without realising it?

The purport is, according to this theory, if there is no one staying on the second moment, then the trouble is, in the first moment he shall have to realise all reals, and in the second moment he shall have to realise their destruction. Then only in the third moment he can say "all reals are momentary". But at that time he himself, being momentary, is not existing. How can he realise the universal momentariness'

Question: Cannot one who has with him the previous impressions *(saṃskārs)* of momentariness, realise and propound the truth of universal momentariness?

Answer: Even then you shall have to believe that the previous impressions and the possessor of them who co-existed, are not momentary, not perished in one moment, and hence only they remained intact to be inherited and to inherit on the successive moments. Here the theory of universal momentariness comes to end. If you say that the impressions (*saṃskārs*) are also momentary, then no effect can be produced in the successive moments on the basis of lost impressions. But we experience the remembrances of past occurrances. This is only possible with the existence of past impressions and their owner. It means that the theory of universal and eternal momentariness is refuted.

(20) The fruits of benevolence etc., mentioned in the Vedas can be possible to occur and to be experienced only if there exists the soul different from the body. The question may arise "If the soul enters the body and leaves the body, then why is it not visible?" The answer to this question is that as already mentioned on account of such thing as a subtle object though it is an entity it is not visible.

(21) In this manner, there is no rule that the activities like the *Yoga* and *Upayoga* and the sensations like desire, *iccha*, *rāga* attachments, passions etc., already explained and the innate joys and sorrows keep decreasing and increasing in consonance with the regeneration or degeneration of the body. From this we can understand that these qualities and nature are not of the body but are of the soul, which is an independent entity different from the body.

(22) There are other proofs also in support of the soul: The remembrance of the previous birth;

(23) The existence of the other words for the "soul" being separate than those of the body;

(24) The fact that if an occasion arises, even the body is sacrificed for our most beloved, and that is our soul. These prove the existence of the soul as different from the body. (If the body was our most beloved, we would not dare sacrifice it. Hence, for whom is the body sacrificed? It is our most beloved soul.)

This logical exposition of the Bhagavān wiped out the doubt of Vayubhuti and he also, along with his five hundred disciples accepted the *charitra dikṣā* at the pious feet of Bhagavān Mahāvīr.

4

THE FOURTH GAṆADHARA: VYAKTA

ARE THE FIVE BASIC ELEMENTS (BHUTAS) REAL?

Now the fourth scholar named Vyakata approached Shri Mahāvīr Bhagavān. Bhagavān himself stated Vyakta's doubt thus "On the basis of such Vedic statement as 'स्वप्नोपमं वै जगत्' meaning the world is illusory like a dream you believed that the five basic elements *(bhụtas)* accepted by people are illusory like a dream and hence they are not real (true). On thẹ other hand, on the basis of such Vedic statements as पृथ्वी देवता, आपो देवता.... etc., (the earth is a deity, water is a deity etc.,) you feel that the five *bhutas* which are emobiments of divinity ought to be real and lasting. Hence emobiments of divinity ought to be real and lasting. Hence, you have entertained the doubt, "Are the five basic elements real or unreal"? When you have such a doubt even regarding the perceptible reality, naturally you might have a greater doubt regarding the soul, which is an imperceptible reality. In other words, you suspect if everything is (are all these things) decidedly void and non-existent?

This argument is given in support of the view that all things are unreal and illusory.

Its logic is all the substances are unreal and illusory, because—

1) Every substance is a mutually relative reality.
2) In this real relationship (the connection) of the reality with the reals is logically impossible.
3) The creation of the real also is logically impossible.
4) The causes producing it are logically impossible.
5) Its visibility also is logically impossible (one which is beyond occurrance).

(1) Existence is relative:

The evidence of the existence or the creation of an object is a relative concept, because an object that is real is evident or accomplished either (i) by itself or (ii) by the relative other object, or (iii) by both, itself and the other relative objects. Now, a substance can be in the form of a cause or an effect. If it produces an effect then only it is called the cause. But first if this causative nature is established, only then this effect can be called an effect. If the cause is not on its own accord evident, then, how can the effect dependent on such a non-evident cause be an established fact? In the same manner, if the effect is not evident by itself, how can the producer dependent on it be styled as cause. In the same manner short and long, far and near, father and son etc., become an established fact only when their mutual relationship and cognition is proved. If the middle finger is proved to be long, then only the ring finger is proved to be short, or if the ring finger is first proved to be short, then only the middle finger can be established as long. The purport is when the objects being dependent on each other are not of their own accord evident, as an established fact, then they cannot be proved to exist even in relation to other objects. Therefore, how can it be proved to exist by itself? Or by its relationship with other things? Or by both?

(2) Is reality different from the real Or not?

In real and existing substances like a pot, etc., there is lying reality or existence. Is this reality or existence different from the substance or not?

(i) If the existence is not different, then it is concluded that "whatever exists is a pot". In other words all things would be existing in the form of a pot. But here you cannot say, "let it be so", because the existence of the pot also is a non-pot, then only can we call it a pot. There being nothing like a non-pot, hence non-pot being unreal, the pot also is proved unreal. That means all things are unreal.

(ii) If reality is different from the object, then the object itself cannot be real. It remains only unreal. In this manner so long as we cannot prove the existence of substances like a non-pot, how can we name an object 'pot'? In other words, like the *'sat'* (existence) or real, there is nothing like *'Abhilāpya'* (a thing which can be expressed by words). The purport is this, the relationship between an object and its existence (reality) being logically impossible to happen, all things are null and void or unreal.

(3) Creation is improbable

In the same manner (i) is a created thing created? or (ii) an uncreated thing is created? or (iii) are both created-uncreated?

(1) The first one is not true, because it is a futile endeavour to create a created one; when a thing has already been created, if it is again created then it will continue to be created endlessly. (2) If you say that the uncreated is created, then that which has not been created is like a horse-horn e.g. unreal. It can never be created. (3) Even the third point is not true because the defects in each of the two appear in both. Now the question is whether there is anything like both the created--uncreated existent or not? If there is such a thing then it results in only one issue of "created only" or "uncreated only". Hence how can there be both? (4) If you say, that one which is in the process of being created, is created" here first of all the question arises "Is the one being produced real? Or unreal?" In this, there is a defect as in the third point since it is self-contradictory. The essence of the argument is this, 'Creation is improbable: therefore, every substance is unreal'.

(4) Is each of causes potential?

An object appears to have been made up from the aggregate of substances, viz. 'Upādān Kārana' and Nimitta kārana (raw material and causative substances). In other words, all things seem to be made out of the aggregate of all the causative substances. But according to your theory of 'all unreal' where there is no such thing as "*all*", what is the meaning of the aggregate of substances? Moreover, if each of these substances does not possess the potentiality for emergence or creation, then how can there be the potentiality of emergence or creation in the whole aggregate? In other words, in the combination of substances when each of which is devoid of the potentiality for creation, how can it be in the causative aggregate present in their combination. If there is no oil in every particle of sand, then it is not present in the mass of sand particles. If there is oil in each sesame grain then only its mass also contains it. Similarly if there is potentiality in every causative substance then each one must be capable of producing an effect. In this manner, since the mass possessing potentiality of causing creation being impossible to exist, each substance in the mass of unreals is also unreal there being the impossibility of the combination of causative substances, everything is unreal.

(5) Visibility impossible

Is the substance visible or invisible? There is nothing like invisible in the world because it is not logically proved. Then there is no visible thing also because it is illogical in this way,

Which is seen is not the whole of the substance but it is only the upward or forward part. This part also being a combination of particles, what we see is not the totality of particles but only the upward or forward part of the particles. There also in the same manner that part is made up of smaller particles and there it will not be wholly seen but only the smallest particles. So think out further and further; only the top most atom will come in your sight, and you call the atom invisible. In this way all things are invisible, all things are non-existent, are unreal.

Now, this is answered.

The refutation of the theory 'सर्वशून्यं' 'All are unreal (null and void)'.

1. First of all, if all things are only *Asat* and unreal, how can this doubt arise, "Are the five elements existing or not?" Because such a doubt cannot arise in the case of objects which are utterly unreal and non-existent like a horse-horn. We do not get this doubt – "Is this a horse-horn or a donkey-horn?" 'Yes, a doubt arises only in the case of things which are true *(Sat)* or real just as, "Is this a stump or a human being?" but not in the case of untrue *(asat)* or unreal substance. Why this difference? Therefore, we say that a thing regarding which a doubt arises is established as *sat* or real. Otherwise why is there not the contrary condition? Just as why is it that we do not doubt unreal objects, and we doubt only real objects? Why does a doubt arise only regarding *'Sat'* or existent reality?

2. If all things are *asat*, untrue, unreal, then the doubt also is proved to be *asat* or untrue.

3. Doubts and illusions are the various forms of *'gyāna'* knowledge and they are connected with the *'gneya'* i.e.

knowable object. But if all things are unreal and non-existent, then there is no difference between what is knowable or what is unknowlable? If everything is unreal then these two contrary conceptions have no meaning.

Question: There is no real thing in a dream, yet we get a doubt regarding it. Do we not?

4) *Answer:* Even in a dream the doubt arises only regarding the previously experienced or heard things. Therefore, even in a dream the cause of a doubt is real *(satya)*. A dream itself being a form of knowledge is dependent on some cause. If a dream is an effect, it is under the principle of cause and effect. If all things are unreal, what can we dream of and why a dream?

5) If all things are unreal and void then why do the following differences arise?

i) One is a dream and the other is non-dream.
ii) One is a truth and the other is a lie.
iii) One is a real city and the other is an illusive city.
iv) One is primary (formal) and the other is secondary (informal).
v) One is an effect and the other is a cause and a creator.
vi) One is *sādhya*, that which is to be accomplished, and other is *sādhana* meaning instrument.
vii) One is the speaker or the spoken subject and the other is utterance.
viii) One is plaintiff and the other is the defendant.
ix) One is a teacher and the other is a disciple.
x) One is a receiver namely the senses, the other is the received such as sound, colour etc.
xi) One is hot and the other is cool.
xii) One is sweet and the other is bitter.
xiii) he earth is always steady; the water is always fluid. Fire is always hot; the wind is always moving. Each of these possesses a particular fixed nature. Why are not they all equal in the form of a dream? Or why are they not real. Why are they not contrary to the natural course? If all things are unreal, untrue, where there is scope for their knowledge in varied forms.

Question: The knowledges relating to them are possible

just like a mirage, but they are not true. The concepts that one is a dream and the other is a non-dream, are mere illusions.

Answer: This cannot be called illusion because knowledge occurs of a thing with regard to a decided particular place, time, and nature etc. in a special form. For instance here the object is silver and there the object is not silver but tin. The pot that existed yesterday is not existent today .... Such knowledge is ture.

6. Is the illusion real or unreal? If the illusion is real then to that extent the real being proved existing in the world, the theory that "all things are unreal" is repudiated. If the illusion itself is unreal, it means that the theory "every knowledge is a dream and that all things are unreal," is false. Consequently the object of knowledge is proved true and real. The knowledge that finds illusion to be unreal is itself real or *sat*. Thus regarding the question "whether all voidness is real or unreal" here also the same difficulty arises.

7. All voidness has to be proved by means of *'Pramāna'* – evidence. If the evidence itself applied to this theory of voidness is real, then the theory of 'All Voidness' becomes false to that extent. If the evidence is unreal, then all voidness cannot be proved as true by such unreal evidence.

Now let us review the first five view-points of the initial or the precedent thesis:

1) If you believe that 'the proof or the evidence of the existence of an object is relative (dependent); and then you say that 'there can be no evidence for the existence of the object', this will be a contradiction. If you say "As per the opinion of only others this is relative", then you have thus accepted 'others', and the 'opinion of others', and they will be proved real and true, not void.

2) "The middle finger is long, the first one is short". In this manner, you first entertain the concepts of actual 'longness' and shortness', and then you say "the long and the short objects because of their mutual relativity are unreal", that is inconsistent.

3) Originally in every object, existence is not merely relative, because existence is in the form of *'Arthakriyākāritva'*.

'Arthakriya' means the action of a substance being created. In other words it means the creation of an effect. Its *'kāritva'*

means its causness, the causative power of a substance. In other words, the power of producing an effect. If long and short as well as similar objects produce effect in the shape of knowledge, they are real, because of their productive power. If they are absolutely unreal, they cannot bring about their knowledge and their cognizable effects.

4) The short finger is called the first finger in comparison with the middle finger, but not in comparison with a sky-flower that is void. Similarly, the first finger is short in comparison with the long finger but not in comparison with a sky-flower, a non-existent object. Similarly, in respect of the middle long finger, the first finger is short, but sky-flower is not called short. From this it is evident that the first finger and the middle finger are real.

5) Since in an object there are countless attributes, *dharmas*, natures, qualities, likewise in it there are also relative *dharmas* like shortness, longness etc., which are real, which are evident and which manifest themselves only when there are helping objects to manifest them. If shortness is not real and if this concept is based merely on relativity then why is there not in the middle long finger, shortness of its own and why is it not known to be so? Hence we shall have to say that in it there is no shortness in respect to its own self, and if that is so, how did we get that concept? In other words shortness is a real entity there, but it is manifested only by comparison with a longer object only (on relativity with another longer object) but not with its own self.

6) If you say that the concepts of shortness and longness arise in respect of each other the question arises —"Do the concepts of both arise simultaneously or gradually"? If you say that they arise simultaneously then the mutual dependence or relativity is lost! 'Dependence or relativity' means the thing on which it depends or the thing with which it is related. It must appear previously in a concept. Here since the point is in regard to the concepts arising at the same time, where is the question of dependance of relativity? If you say that both concepts emerge gradually, it means that either of these arising concepts of 'shortness' or 'longness' will be considered as arising without dependence. From this it means that the concepts of shortness or longness are self-arising but not arising dependently. Even our experience is such that on

the accumulation of all causes like sense-contact etc., the knowledge of objects like a pot etc., arise independently, and this knowledge has arisen without any dependence on other objects, and this is an established fact according to our experience. A child just at the time of its birth would acquire the first knowledge only thus without dependence. Therefore this theory that the realisation or knowledge is always relatively dependent is wrong. Otherwise if two things are not short and long and if they are equal how can there be the mutual expectation between such things just as there can be no mutual dependence between the two eyes.

7) Therefore say that in a substance there are two sorts of forms viz.,

Independent form, and dependent form. The existence, individuality, the realness, colour, taste etc., are independent forms, 'indepednent' in this sense that they are existing and knowable (cognizable) of their own accord, but not dependent upon others. Thus such independent forms of substance are self existing and self cognizable – comprehensive of their own accord. In other words to know these we have not to depend upon any relative. They are known themselves meaning without any relation to others. As for example, we know that the finger exists– it is real. In it there are various forms like existence, realness, pink colour, red colour, etc. We know each of these without depending upon any relative. We don't ask here 'The finger has existence and realness in what respect in whose relation?' No, nothing of the sort; existence means existence, redness means redness. The finger is existent of its own accord, the finger is reddish of its own accord. But if the curiosity arises to know is the finger short or long, then the question arises 'You are asking short or long in what respect, in whose relation?'

Here comes the second category of dependent form. 'Dependent' in this sense that to know shortness or longness we have to depend thus upon another relative aspect to be known. 'In whose relation this finger is asked whether to be short or long'. If the question is of the first finger, then we can say that it is short in relation with the second finger, which is long in respect of the first finger'. Thus the concept of the form of shortness in the first finger is dependent on the concept of the longness in the second finger and vice versa.

Say shortness and longness to be known are mutually dependent. It means that they are not self-cognizable but are cognizable (comprehensive) only with respect to others. In other words for the knowledge of such forms like shortness and longness, we have to depend upon knowing the other relative aspect and its comparative form.

In this manner, in a substance the forms like shortness, longness etc., are dependant on their opponent relative aspect to be known, whereas the forms like existence, individuality, colour, etc., are independent forms irrespective of any relative aspect to be known.

Now, when there is no necessity for any relative aspect to be known in the case of such independent forms like existence etc., and as they are self cognizable (means known and dealt with independently) the theory that "because in this world everything being dependent is null and void" is repudiated. That means it is proved baseless. In other words the substances are real and also their forms like existence and colour etc., are real, but not void, not illusive like a dream's objects. Even the dependent forms like shortness-longness are also real; but only forms cognizability depends upon other relative aspects. In short, the theory of all void is itself void, known without any despendence but yet on account of our desire for knowing and for outward comparison for the other dependent qualities, we try to know them by means of comparison as short and long. In this manner, if an object has in itself such independent qualities as reality, colour, taste etc., then knowledge, in the absence of comparison is not void. Therefore the theory of "All being void" is baseless.

8) If the existence of anything like shortness etc., is not independent viz. not self-established then the existence of the short object also will not be independent, but dependent on others. Now don't say let it be dependent, because where there is no concept of comparison with a long finger, atleast there remains the reality that 'this is a finger', and the concept and existence of longness also will be lost inasmuch as there is the absence of a comparison with a short finger. In other words, there is a total loss of all conceptual significations and all the things possessing relative qualities which you believe as void'! But that is not seen. In that time also, which is devoid of any comparison, there do exist short and long objects as

they were and are seen also necessarily. From this, independent existence of real objects is proved.

9) If all are unreal, then even the relativity of shortness and longness will be proved unreal. If so, how can this distinction be made? How can the dealing of short and long will prevail and how can they be authenticated?

Question: The nature of things is such that they are dealt with as short and long relatively in relation with others, and you can say that 'then unreality being the same, why is the long not treated or dealt with as the short'. The reason is that this is the nature of the thing. A question is improper regarding nature.

Answer. Very good, then, from this idea of *swabhāva* of the thing, which means the nature of ownself not of the other, it is deduced that the thing is *'sat'* namely real, by accepting separately the ownself and the other. In consequence it amounts to a refutation of *sarvaśunyatā* viz. all-voidness, absolute nihilism.

10) The process of being one thing relative to the other comprises four items:

i) the individual person knowing this process of relativity;

ii) the action of being relative;

iii) the thing to which the object is related; and

iv) the relative object.

Now if all these are unreal, then nothing of these remain individually special, just as 'this is a person, but not an object'. If each of these possesses the specialities of being a person, or of being an object, or of being the process of relativity etc., in other words, if the differentiated speciality is attached to each one, it means that they are real, because in 'all unreal', this differentiated speciality cannot be attached to anyone. Consequently the theory of absolute nihilism is refuted, broken to pieces so to say.

Summary:

In this world, objects are of our kinds:

1) स्वत:सिद्ध,—*swataḥ siddha* created of its own accord, without a creator, such as the special creations like clouds that arise without a creator.

2) परत:सिद्ध,— *parataḥ siddha* (created by a creator) just as

the pots etc., created by a potter etc.

3) उभयतः सिद्ध,— *ubhayataḥ siddha* (created by both one's ownself and the sons etc., born by the couple and by one's own *karmas.*

4) नित्यसिद्ध,— *nitya siddha* (ever existent), like the sky etc. This *siddha* (accomplished) is from the point of view of creation. From the point of view of knowledge, 'The pot' is self cognizable. It means, it is knowledge without the knowledge of any relatives. Whereas shortness and longness are evident dependently (viz. knowable only on knowing its relative concept.) This differentiation is not consistent with the nihilistic theory (*sarva-śunyatā*) self cognizable self-comprehensive.

The Relationship between a Substance and its Existence:

1) First if you accept the existence of the pot, "The pot exists" but not as 'it does not exist', and thus after accepting the pot as existent then if you ask the question "what is the relationship between the pot and its existence", then by such question, non-existence or unreality of both is not proved; otherwise why does not such a question arise in repect of unreal "Donkey-horns"?

2. You say that a pot is unreal and non-existent. There also the similar question arises: what is the relation between the pot and non-existence?

(i) If a pot and non-existence are one and the same, in other words the non-existence is not different from the pot, then only the pot remains, only the pot is accepted, but a separate entity like *"Asatta"* unrealness is not proved.

(ii) If you say both of them are different, a separate entity of a thing like non-existence is not sound, hence it is baseless.

3. If you are a nihilist, when you know and speak of nihilism are your words and knowledge of speaking and knowing of your nihilism different from you? Or are they not different from you? If you say that they are not different (like the tree and the mango which are not different then you being not void, not unreal like horse-horn the existence of knowledge and utterance also is proved to be true. If you say that they are different from you, then you being different from this knowledge and utterance, you yourself are proved ignorant

and dumb, and as such how can you prove about your nihilism?

4. Regarding the pot and its existence, the existence is the dharma quality-attribute or nature of the pot. The nature of the pot is not different from its container pot, and is different from clothes etc. Just as the existence of pot is a different entity, so the existences of clothes etc., are different entities. Then where is the problem of oneness of all these? Every existence of every object is different. Therefore, "Whatever exists is a pot", this rule is wrong. If it is asked "What is here? Pot or non-pot?" then you will have to say "Pot". What is a pot? It is existent. Just as what is here? Mango or something else. In answer we will have to say "Mango". What is a mango? Is it a tree or something else. Then it will be said it is a tree. So just like mangoes, separate and mutually different existence are established.

1) Of the four alternatives, regarding the *utpanna* (created) there is a particular decided one fact.

First of all you place four alternatives for a thing taking birth in this way; a thing takes birth in which position; the thing itself being created; uncreated; Both created–uncreated or in the process of creation?

Now we would ask, are these four alternatives 'created' on or uncreated ones? As regards the first point of 'created one' the alternative is meaningless, because how can we ask about a created one if a created one takes birth? If you apply alternatives in the case of the 'non-created one, why don't you place such alternative in respect of the non-existent ones like sky-flowers which are also uncreated?

2) In respect of objects like a pot, the question is, if they are not at all created at any time, why is it so that they are seen only after the aggregation of the causes like a potter etc., and not before that? In the same manner afterwards when broken by means of a stick etc., why are they not seen? If they are always uncreated like sky-flowers, the unseen should always remain unseen.

3) If the knowledge and statements of voidness are absolutely uncreated, who gave the expression to voidness?

4) The real condition is that a pot being newly created— a pot taking birth from one point of view is partially created. From another point of view it is partially uncreated. From a third, it is both partially created and partially uncreated. From

the fourth point of view, it is partially in the process of being created, and takes birth. This can be clarified thus:

(i) The pot before birth is in the form of clay, and the clay is already *'utpanna'* a created one. So pot also in its form can be called 'created' *(Utpanna)*. (ii) The pot before birth is not of pot-shape. So it can be called 'Uncreated' (*Anutpanna*) as per that shape. (iii) By these two aspects of clay and shape a pot can be called 'created and uncreated' *(Ubhay)*. (iv) The pot just in the process of creation can be called being created (*Utpadyamāṇa*).

In respect of these four alternatives, it can be said that *the pot takes birth,* already created, uncreated, created and uncreated both, and being in the process of creation.

Here the Jain theory of *Anekāntvād—sāpekshvād,* in other words the theory of relativity is to be taken into consideration. According to *anekāntvād*, clay form and particular shape are different and not different from the pot; different in some respect and not different from another respect. Here the four alternatives are taken upon the 'not different' point., e.g. pot is clay itself, hence clay being created already, the pot also is considered as created.

The pot newly taking birth first as partially created while it is in the form of clay; and takes birth in a special form first as an uncreated one because the pot is *abhinna*, not different from clay and its special form (round shape). Thinking of existence it is existent first in the form of clay; it means the pot exists. So long as it has no special form, then it is not existent in that form with relationship to form and shape both '*ubhay*' i.e., "created – uncreated"; and from the point of view of the present time, it is while in the process of creation created also otherwise the process would be fruitless, if considered as not created.

Whereas, the pot that has already been created, now does not exist in the four alternatives namely created, uncreated, both; and in the process of being created. Because '*Sva-dravya*' the self-substance has been created in the form of a pot; and 'Sva-paryāya self modifications as round, red, large, light etc., has already been created. So now what to talk of to be created. And the *pardravya* (the other substance) cannot emerge here in the form of a cloth or in the form of non-self modification. In other words, it cannot assume another form; otherwise it would be in another's form. The summary is this. The question of creation regarding a pot that has already been created is useless. Similarly, it is also useless to ask if a created thing is at present uncreated? Or created-uncreated or in the process of being created. If we put the same four questions about an object in the process of being created, we would say that it is not created *par-rūp* in the non-self form. In this manner, the sky which is always existent, will not be created in any one of the four forms. Thus the uncreated one also, the pot is always existent in the form of *Svadravya* (own substance). So in that form it is not to be created anew.

This is about a pot and the sky in the original *svadravya* form or as regards modification they cannot be created in any of the four alternative forms in their non-self modifications. Even that which has been created in its own *paryaya* (self-modification) cannot be created now in that *'Svuparyaya'*; and can be created in an uncreated *'sva-paryaya'* self-modification.

1) The productive causative aggregation can be logical and established

'Since all is void, there is nothing existent like such things as causative substances'. This statement of yours is illogical and is contradicted because at first it is clearly evident that this statement has been produced by such substances as throat, lips and the palate etc. When that is so, it is nonsense to say that there are no such things as causative aggregations.

Question: This appears to be so because of *Avidya*= false conception) illusion, because it has been said,

काम-स्वप्न-भयोन्मादैरविद्योप्लवात् तथा ।
पश्यन्त्यसन्तमप्यर्थं जनः केशेन्दुकादिवत् । ।

On account of severe sensuality, lust, dream, fear and infatuation (मतिभ्रम) and illusion, people see before their eyes unreal thing and deem it *sat* like the thread-like illusory hair as real.

Answer: If all causative aggregations notwithstanding their being unreal, *(asat)* are perceived, why is it that the causative aggregations of the tortoise-hair or the donkey horn are not perceived as substances? They are not seen because they are unreal. Is that not so? Therefore, whatever causative substances we see are real.

2) The causative aggregative substances *(sāmagri)* like the

chest, the head, the throat etc., the speaker, sentences comprising sounds, and the subject expressed. Are they existent or not? If they are existent then how can you say that all is void? If they are non-existent, then who heard "*Sarvamśunyaṃ*" All voidness? In the same manner, the meaning of 'mother' is one who has children; how can she be barren? The utterance is that which is said how can it be devoid of propounded subject matter?

3) *Question:* The speaker, the utterance etc., nothing of them is real. Therefore, the propounded matter also is not real. In this manner voidness of all cannot be propounded.

Answer: Not at all. Tell me whether the utterance of such theory is true, or false. If true, then this itself is proved real. If false, it being devoid of authenticity, the idea expressed by it namely '*sarvaśunyatā*' is proved baseless.

4) If you say, "we have accepted this utterance of whatever kind?" Is this acceptance true or false? Moreover in the principle of *sarvaśunyatā* what are the acceptor, the acceptance and the accepted principles?

5) If all are unreal (*asat*), then the fixed particular dealings and denotations will be lost or proved false or they will be unauthentic, baseless, unproved and illogical. Why does oil emerge from only such causative substances as the sesame? Why not from sand? Why is not any effect produced from the sky-lotus? Why only between particular substances are seen the relationship of cause and effect but not between others? These particular occurrances are not possible to occur from void substances, but from real substances with varied particular natures. Then only they are possible to occur or be created.

6) At the same time to say that 'all are in the form of causative aggregations, all are born of causative aggregations', is also not proper. It is contradictory because the atoms are not created by anything, still they are proved by the visible gross effect. Such is the actual situation in fact. Otherwise to say that all are born out of aggregations – and afterwards to say that "the atom is not born," is just like saying "all utterance is untrue". This saying is refuted by your own statement, because the atoms consist of the aggregates. If there are no atoms at all as the basis, how could molecules etc., be created without causative aggregations? If you

consider that even atoms are created, then the question arises–'from what basic substances are they created'? Creation cannot take place out of void otherwise there will be no particular condition and position there being no particularity in void.

7) The hind side of a thing being not visible is void and is non-existent.

1) "The hind side of a thing cannot be seen hence it is not existing. When there does not exist the hind side, there is nothing like the front side. So the front side is also not existent". What kind of inference is this? On the contrary on the vision of the fore side of it, the hind side is proved.

Because there is a hind side, then only a certain part called fore side is there. If there is no hind side, what is the meaning of the fore side?

Therefore, when on the basis of the existence of the fore side by the inference the existence of the hind side is logically established, then by refuting it your proposition of the frontside goes contradictory to your own statement. When you deny the hind side, your statement— that there is a fore side– is refuted. The hind-side goes parallel with the front side. To refute the hind side, would mean to refute the front side and hence the statement of front side is self contradictory.

2) You said that "because only the front side of the object is visible, the object is not existent". In this statement, the words, "visible" and "not existent" are contradictory. If you say that it is visible out of illusion, then the question is why is it that front side of the sky-flower is not visible?

3) If there is '*Sarwam śūnyam*' (total voidness) then how can there be differences like modern and old, near and distant, front and back? If you say that-the front, back and distant are denoted according to the opponent's opinion–then the question arises: is there a difference between "Own" opinion and "opponent's" opinion? Is there anything like real opinion and void opinion? In the same manner if you accept (treat) this difference as real, it means the repudiation of 'the theory of total voidness. If it is not accepted and if still the dealing, the denotation continues, why do not such dealing and denotation prevail in respect of 'sky-flowers' also?

4) If all things are unreal, why like the back side of a thing the front side also is not invisible? Why are not all sides invisible? Or why are not all sides visible or, why is it that the front is seen but not the back?

5) In the things like *sfatik* etc., through the transparent items the hind side also is visible. Since this much is proved, consequently all did not remain void, hence your theory "all is void" is not correct. If you say that even this is unreal, then for proving the theory of '*sarva śūnyatva* all voidness you have forwarded as its reason back portion is invisible, but this reason is wrong. The reason to be forwarded should be "all is invisible" but that is a contradiction. Otherwise you could have said because the totality is invisible, so the totality is unreal." Having trust on this "all unreal", if you walk on closing your eyes, it is possible that you might proceed towards a wall or a well and there you might fall into the well or dash against the wall.

6) "The hind side being invisible is not existent". If you say so, at least you accept that the front is visible. Therefore atleast the existence of the senses (as the means of perceiving) and the objects of the senses is proved. If even these are unreal then the distinction between perceptible things and imperceptible things cannot be logically established.

7) Even invisible things are existing and are not unreal. Even the doubt regarding unreal things "Are all unreal or real?" itself is an existing real thing. If this doubt also is unreal, what about the object of the doubt namely what about *sarwasūnyatva?* If you say even doubt is unreal, it means there is no doubt regarding the five elements. If that is so, the five elements are proved to be real and existent. Now you see that though the back portion is invisible, its existence is proved by inference. In this world, the existence of many things is proved by inference.

The Illustration of Invisible things proved to be Existent by means of Inference

The wind is cognizable (is understandable) through touch, sound, calmness, shaking etc., and as the possessor of the qualities like coolness, movement etc. When we are touched by the cool breezes of wind, we say, "the cool wind is blowing". The sound is visible in the direction of the wind but not in the opposite direction. From this, it is by inference established that the wind that is the resort of the sound is blowing in that direction.

The sky is an established fact as the basis for the earth and water. The earth has a basis because it has a form. Just as earth is the base for water, the sky is the basis for the earth. The five basic elements are proved by the bodies of the souls and their utility.

The five basic elements are evident as the support of soul's body and their utility.

Vanaspatikāya (Vegetative Body):

Like the body of a human being even the *vanaspati kāya* has birth, old age, life, death and growth. Even after it is cut, it has similar physical creation of sprouting, cherishing desires, treatment etc., hence it is proved to be a living thing. The existence of a soul in *vanaspati kāya* is proved thus:

1) Touch me not sensitive plant—Bashful	Proved by its contraction at touch
2) Wood apple—a creeping plant	proved by its dependence for its safety on a hedge or a wall.
3) Shami, etc.	proved by sleep, waking, and contraction.
4) Bakula, a perfumed plant	proved by the attraction of sound.
5) The Ashoka tree—Jonecia Ashoka	proved by the attraction of form.
6) Kurubaru	proved by the attraction of scent.
7) Virahak	proved by the attration of taste.
8) Champa Tilak	proved by the attraction of touch.

The *Prithvi kāya jiva* is like a muscular sprout.

It is proved by the growth of the sprouts of the same species, after having been formerly cut. The dug out mountain, or mine, gets filled up in the same form after many years. How can this happen without a soul?

The *apkāya jiva*, like a frog, coming out from dug out earth by its natural manifestation, is proved animate. It is evidently animate like a fish falling from the sky clouds etc. by their distortions.

The *vāyukāya jiva* like bullock without other's direction, makes irregular horizontal movement, so it has soul.

The *agnikāya jiva*. It is evident as animate from its living on food (fuel) and increase with the availability of sufficient food and by its consequent development.

In this manner, the elements like earth etc., are different from the distortions of the sky like twilight and have form. Therefore, they are *jivakāyas* soul's bodies. If in the world there were no souls possessing one sense, the (*saṃsār*) the world itself would have ended because from times immemorial the process of souls attaining *mokṣa* (salvation) is current. Yet there is no end to souls. If so, where were all these souls staying? Here we should believe that they all were lying in the '*ekendrīya*' bodies.

Where is Violence, Or Non Violence

Question: Then in this world pervaded with *jivas,* how can non-violence be observed?

Answer: The earth etc., which are destroyed by weapons lack life; therefore in utilising them there is no violence. In the same manner, even this is proper to be known that according to the '*Nischayinay*' there is no rule that "there is necessarily violence, if the *jiva* dies; and necessarily non-violence where the *jiva* does not die." Even this is not a rule that if *jivas* are less, there is non-voilence, and if *jivas* are more there is violence", because those wicked people, who have the evil motive of killing a king etc., are violent though they do not kill them. Likewise a doctor though he might give pain to a patient is necessarily non-violent. The enlightened *Munis* who observe five '*samitis*' (awareness of sinlessness) and three '*Guptis*' (mental-vocal-physical auspicious activities accompanied with the restraint over inauspicious activities), know the nature of *jivas*. Over and above they are always cautious and careful in their concern for total non-violence to *jivas*, and always pursue that objective. Now even if at any time violence might have been committed by them under awareness of *samitis-guptis*, they are not violent. On the contrary in any activity with non-cautious mental mood, even if a *jiva* does not die, there is violence because of the absence of caution and awareness for protection of *jivas*.

Therefore in fact the the inauspicious mental attitude is violence, just as *Tandulia Matsyas* etc., are bound by the *karmas* of violence only on account of thoughts of violence, even though they are not actually comitting violence. Who is this *Tandulia Matsya*! It is a very small fish staying in the eye brow of a big gigantic fish. It sees that "along with a big wave of water a lot of small fish enter the cave-like open mouth of that very big fish lying in sleep": and it thinks "how lucky this big fish is to have this big lot of fishes easily available directly in mouth for devouring." Afterwards on returning the water wave out, those small fishes are thrown out intact alive. Looking this the small *Tandulia* fish thinks, "oh! how foolish this big fish is to leave up such a big lot of fishes without eating them! If I were in its place, I would have eaten all the fishes, and I would not have left off a single of them."

These thoughts of violence will be tantamout to actual violence inasmuch as it binds the *karmas* of violence which send that jiva to hell!

Question: Is not violence the actual killing of the external *jiva*?

Answer: There is *anekāntvād* i.e., it may or may not be violence. If the external killing of a *jiva* is a cause or an effect of inauspicious conscience (mentality) it is no violence. If there is no inauspicious mentality it is no violence. Just as on account of the purity of the mental mood i.e., sanctity of the heart of one who is free from *moha* (insanity).

Thus the five elements (bhutas) are real but not unreal. Out of these, first four are having conciousness and the last one Ākāsh (Sky) does not possess conciousness.

The proposition, "the whole *saṃsār* is like a dream" is to show to the *Bhavya jivas* the worthlessness of money, women, sons, worldly objects etc. On hearing this they may leave off their blind avarice and affections in them and get indifferent towards them and consequently make efforts for salvation.

In this manner having been relieved of all his doubts brahmin Vyakta with his 500 disciples accepted *Charitra-dharma* on the spot at the hands of Bhagavān Mahāvīr.

5
THE FIFTH GAṆADHARA: SUDHARMA
IS THE BIRTH SIMILAR?

Does the *jiva* take the same form in the next birth as it had in this birth? This was the doubt of the fifth Brahmin named Sudharma.

Bhagavān Mahāvīr Swami said to him "You learnt from the Vedic statement that *'pūrūśo vai pūrūsatva masaśnute pasavah pasūtvam*," "पुरुषो वै पुरुषत्वमश्नुते पशवः पशुत्वम्" It means "human beings take birth as human beings in their next life, and animals as animals". You also learnt from this Vedic statement, "श्रृगालो वै जायते यः सपुरीषो दह्यते" It means the one whose body is burnt along with excrement is born as a jackal. Thus we learn that human beings also can take birth as jackals. therefore, you have entertained this doubt.

The Arguments relating to a Similar Dissimilar next Birth:

1) In supporting the view that the *jiva* takes birth in the next life in the same kind as it is in this life, it is argued "Wheat grows from wheat, maize from maize, mango from mango. Thus the effect is created in accordance with the cause". But this kind of belief is not logically sensible, because an arrow can be made out of a horn: and if it is sown after being smeared with particular oil, grass also grows therefrom. In the shastra called *'Yoni Praabhrit'* it is said that from the combination of many diverse substances snakes, lions, gold, pearls can be created. In practical life we find that scorpions take birth from scorpions, as well as from cowdung.

2) The theory is that the effect is created only in accordance with the seed. Now according to this principle also *jiva* can take a different kind of birth in the next life. It happens in this manner; In *saṃsār*, the seed of the next life is *karma*, and these *karmas*, are created in strange forms due to the strangeness of the causes such as *Mithyatva* (false faith) and *'avirati'* (lack of refrainment) etc. Then the sprouts of

next life that arise from these strange *karmas* also remain different in '*Gati*' (human existence, beastly existence etc.,); '*Jati*' (from 'one-sense' life to 'five-sense' life), strength, wealth, appearance etc., what wonder is there in this? By inference; the worldly births of the *Jiva* are varied in the form of inhabitants in hell, beasts, etc. Because this is the effect of strange *karmas*. The different effects of *karmas* is like the worldly differences that arise from agriculture or trade etc., as occupations. The implication is that in the world, the birth is not accidental; but is the fruit of previous *karmas*. The rule is therefore as is the *karma*; so is the kind of birth. *Karmas* of the similar kind produce the similar kind of birth; and dissimilar ones produce dissimilar kind of birth.

3) The ripening of *karmas* is strange because it is in the form of modification of pudgals i.e. (effect in the form of inanimate substances). For this, similar illustration is of the cloud etc., and opposite illustration is of the sky. For the creation of clouds strange causes happen hence there is strangeness in clouds. Whereas for the sky there are no strange causes, hence there is no strangeness in the sky. As regards *karma* special strangeness happens on account of many sorts of *Āvarans* (veils). If the cause is strange, the effect must be strange. This is quite logical.

4) You say 'the next birth is created always of the same type as of the present; but this is not proper, because for the next birth, only this birth is not the seed, but the seed is, this birth with all its auspicious and inauspicious actions and activities. Man performs in this life strange activities and these are not futile. We must therefore, have to believe that a strange kind of birth appears, as their fruit.

5 *Question:* In actions relating to such things as cultivating fields etc. the fruit is visible and direct, but the actions like violence and knowledge ceremony are performed only according to one's choice and mental tastes and hence they are fruitless. It means that they do not attribute anything to the next life. How can there be a different kind of life in the next birth?

Answer: If action like violence and knowledge are fruitless:

i) There is the difficulty of '*Kritanash*' and '*Akrutāgam*' namely there is the danger of a noble action that has been done here going fruitless and the danger of good or bad fruits being obtained here even though one has not done anything good or bad in the previous life.

ii) Even the next birth will not be possible because in this world the cause of birth is *karma,* and you do not believe in *karmas* being produced from the activities of life, studying scriptures non-violence etc. Now when there is no next birth at all, where is the question of a rebirth of the same kind as of this life? Yet if there is the next birth, then it is '*Krit-Āgam*' namely the coming of the fruit of the previous actions done. In this manner birth from birth continues endlessly, the soul will never be emancipated from it, and *mokṣa* will never be attained, because according to your theory the previous birth only is the cause for the next birth.

In short, you do not attach any importance to the actions of present life as the other causes. You believe only in the previous birth as the cause, and that results in infinite births.

6) *Question:* From clay, its equivalent effect in the form of a pot appears in clay's own nature. In the same manner from this life by its own nature why cannot the same kind of life emerge in the next birth?

Answer: The pot over and above the nature of clay depends also upon the doer, implements etc. In the same manner here the next birth depends upon *karmas*. If the next birth appears by its own nature but not by *karmas* then the body of the next life would be of unfixed form like clouds. How could it be of particular form?

7) If you say "By its own nature the present life generates the similar next birth", then the question arises what do you mean by the 'own nature of the thing'?

(i) It is the thing itself;

(ii) or causelessness or;

(iii) the quality of the things.

(1) If you mean by 'the thing itself the present birth, then that is destroyed even before the next birth. So how can it be a cause for the next life as its nature? If you deem this thing as the cause can it be a cause for itself?

(2) If you 'by own nature of the thing' mean causelesness, then this difficulty arises. The next birth due to causelessness becomes of the same kind as this. Now if only causelessness is effective for creating the next birth, these questions arise:

Questions on causedness:

(i) Why is it that the next birth should be of the same kind? But not dissimilar?

(ii) Why should not there be an end to the *saṃsār* i.e. the cycle of births and deaths!

(iii) Why should there be a particular shape?

(iv) And the birth should be always real or always unreal, but why real only for a particular time?

3) If you mean by 'own nature of the thing' (*vastu dharma*') then this point comes up 'the present birth' by its *Vastu dharma* makes the next birth of the same kind'. If so the question is what *dharma* of this life becomes cause for the next life? Does this *dharma* possess a form or is it formless? You cannot say 'formless', because the effect of a formless thing cannot be form-possessing thing like *body*, sorrows, joys etc. If you mean by 'own nature of the thing', form-possessing substance , then how can this principle be made that 'it should create always similar *dharma*?' So we can say that this life gives rise to only a similar next birth.

4) The actual situation is this. The next birth is a modification of the soul. Such varied modifications happen not only in the case of soul, but in the three worlds, everything remains as it is with many modifications unchanged, and gets changed with many newly created modifications. These modifications being "inseparable" from the substance, we can say a substance goes on being created in the form of successive modifications leaving previous modifications. Now the question arises where is the rule that those newly created modifications must be only similar and not dissimilar to the previous ones'? When there is no such rule, then why should you insist upon the same kind of next birth? Even in this life just as many similar modifications like existence, soulhood etc. remain as they are, in the same way many dissimilar modifications like childhood, youth etc., happen as different; there also, why do you not insist upon similar modifications namely those of the same kind?

Question: We speak of similarity only pertaining to manhood and animalhood etc.

Answer: You should bear in mind that the creation of modifications is dependent on the cause. Similar causes generate similar modifications, and dissimilar causes generate dissimilar modifications. In the running matter the causative *karmas* are strange also, therefore the modifictions like the next life etc., created by these strange *karmas* will be dissimilar also. Otherwise why only for manhood? One who is poor here (in this life) will be poor in the next life, a rich man will be rich, a sick man will be sick, and one of low birth will be one of low birth only. But you cannot say "Oh it is definitely so" because in such happenings the austerities like *tapasyā*, penance, charity and meditation etc., would be fruitless. Even in the present life a sick man can become healthy; a poor man can become a rich man. If dissimilar can happen in this birth, why should not be the next birth dissimilar also?

5) If the next birth is of the same kind, the Vedic statement like "शृगालो वै एष.....अग्निहोत्रं स्वर्गकामः" "*"Shrigalo Vai Esh....." "Agnihotram Swarge-Kāmah"* etc. will be proved meaningless! So "पुरुषो वै पुरुषत्वम्....." its meaning is this: one who is by nature good, polite, kind can again take similar birth as a man by earning here again, the *karma* of the life-span of manhood for the next life, through these qualities.

Sudharma also became fully free from his doubts by this explanation of Bhagavān Mahāvīr paramātmā and became a disciple of the Bhagavān with his 500 pupils.

6

THE SIXTH GAṆADHARA: MANDIT

ARE THERE BONDAGE AND DELIVERANCE?

The (sixth) brahmin by name Mandit came. The Bhagavān said to him, "You have the doubt whether the soul undergoes bondage and *mokṣa* or not? You have found two kinds of vedic statements"

(i) स एष विगुणो विभुर्न बध्यते न संसरति न मुच्यते मोचयति वा....

(ii) न ह वै सशरीरस्य प्रियाप्रिययोरपहतिरस्ति....

The first statement means, "This all pervasive soul '*Viguno*' devoid of the three attributes- 'Satva' 'Rajas' 'Tamas' never comes into bondage; does not undergo transformation in the *saṃsār*; does not attain *mokṣa*; nor does cause deliverance of others" Whereas the second statement means, "There is no voidness of joys and sorrows in the soul possessing body. The soul becomes bound in the body. It also experiences the changes in joys and sorrows, and when it gets permanent deliverance from the body, then this botheration ends this series of entanglement ends". From this, you have entertained the doubt whether the soul should have bondages and *mokṣa* or not.

'Poorva Paksha' :-Opponent's view: His proposition 'Bondage and *Moksa* (deliverance) do not exist.

The soul has no bondage. In support of this theory, the idea arises, "Bondage means the binding of the soul with *karmas*". But the question is, "do the soul and *karmas* coexist or do they come successively?"

1) If the soul is first and karma next, then this cannot happen i.e., it is not logically possible because in that state either the soul might have taken birth without cause or the soul might have been in existence from times immemorial. But in the first alternative it is impossible, because without a cause an effect cannot be created. That which is created is preceded by a cause, and if it is created without a cause, then it may just perish without a cause, and perished after being created, how could it be visible at all?

1) If the soul is first and *karma* next, then this cannot existence without cause and how did they stick (cling) to the soul? If they cling thus, namely without the cause, then to the delivered souls they may cling!

2) If *karmas* are first and *jiva* next, even this cannot be possible because without a doer how can *karmas* be created at all? If they are created thus, then they might perish without any cause!

3) If you say that *karmas* and soul are created together, then there are defects on both the sides. Moreover between these two there will not be possible even the logical link of doer and deed, just as between the left and right horn created at the same time, this relationship of a doer and a deed does not exist.

In this manner, the bondage of the soul and *karma* is not logically possible. If the soul is not at all in bondage, consequently how can there be deliverance? If there is the union between *karmas* and the soul from times immemorial, then that union without a beginning would be ever-lasting which means the union cannot be destroyed. Hence deliverance *(mokṣa)* cannot be logically possible. Will the union between the soul and the sky, which is without beginning get ever destroyed? The implication is that the soul has neither bondage nor deliverance (*mokṣa*).

The Refuting View: Bondage and Deliverance (Mokṣa) do exist

1) The series of the body and the *karmas* is without a beginning like the series of the seed and the fruit. Without a cause, there can be no effect. Therefore this is to be accepted that *karmas* have been created by the causative soul in some previous body. That body has been formed by the causative *karmas* done previously......In this manner, the chain between *karmas* and body is infinite. But it should be remembered that *karmas* and the body are both causes and means, whereas the doer of *karmas* and body is the soul. For the soul to do *karmas* the body is the means: and to create the body, *karmas* are the means. In this manner, *karmas* in series remain clung to the soul. Therefore the bondage on the soul is proved.

Question: If *karmas* exist, should they not be visible? If not visible how can their existence be believed in?

Answer: Let the *karmas* be invisible and imperceptible by the senses, but their existence is inferred on the basis of their effect. Otherwise if we think in this manner, just because your intelligence is not visible, does it mean that it does not exist? Are you devoid of intelligence? There is no rule that a thing that is not visible does not exist.

2) There cannot be an end to an ever-existing phenomena. But this is not an absolute truth. That 'which is without a beginning cannot perish'. This kind of one-sided view is not sound (not established by an evidence). The series of *karma-saṃyog* (karma-binding) which is without a beginning, can come to an end. As for instance, if the seed is dried or if the fruit is burnt, its series of seed and fruit which has been running from the times immemorial and which is without a beginning comes to an end. If a son remains bachelor and observes celibacy throughout his life, his series of father and son, father and son, father and son running from the times immemorial, will come now to an end. If the hen dies before hatching eggs, or if the egg is destroyed, then its series ends, because it does not further continue. Therefore,though the series of the union between gold and clay has been in existence from the time of their existence, but by means of its burning in fire etc., the series of their union ends. In the same manner, by means of non-violence, self-restraint and austerities the union of soul with *karma* also ends, and deliverance (salvation, *mokṣa*) is attained. This is a fact that – deliverance is possible only of the "*bhavya jivas*', but not of the '*abhavya jivas*. 'Bhavyas' i.e. those souls that are worthy of salvation (eligible for attaining salvation).

What is Bhavyatva? How?

Question: Why is it that some are *bhavya* souls and some are *abhavya* souls? If you say that this difference is like the difference between the inhabitants of hell and animals, then it becomes evident that the difference is caused by *karmas*.

Answer: No. There is a difference on account of nature. Though all the substances are equal being *sat* (real), yet by nature some substances are animate (conscious) and some are inanimate. This difference is from the times immemorial; and due to such varied nature of those substances, naturally some of them are animate and some are inanimate. In the same manner, though all souls are equal as regards conscience naturally some are *bhavyas* (worthy of salvation) and the others are *abhavyas* (unworthy of the salvation). This difference has been in existence from times immemorial. The series has no beginning. But when a *bhavya* soul achieves salvation, its *bhavyatva* is ended.

Question: If the eligibility (worthiness) of salvation *bhavyatva* like the soulhood is natural, then that is ever-existing. Why should it end or perish! Just as *jivatva* does not end, why should *Bhavyatva* end (be destroyed)?

Answer: Though '*ghat-pragabhav*' (i.e. true previous absent state of the pot before its birth) is without a beginning as soon as its effect the pot takes birth i.e. comes into existence, the '*ghat-pragabhav*' i.e. the absent state is destroyed. In the same manner, as soon as the salvation as the effect of *bhavyatva* is attained, *bhavyatva* perishes. This is quite logical. Do not say that *pragabhav* is of an absence state and *bhavyatva* is of a non-absent state, hence how can the *bhavyatva* be compared to *pragabhav*?"

Because even *pragabhav*, when the pot is in the state of being created (namely, is in the process of creation) is in the form of a special combination of clay-pudgals (specially shaped clay-bulk) and pot is to some extent existent in that form. Though *pragabhav* in the form of previous absence is without a beginning, it can perish in the form of clay bulk. *Bhavyatva* being the eligibility of attaining salvation comes to an end immediately after salvation is attained, because a soul after attaining salvation is not eligible for salvation. The clay transformed into pot is not now called eligible for pot. Hence now the intended very effect is there, but not its eligibility.

As per *anekāntvād*, a *pragabhāva* is not absolutely in the form of absent state only of a substance but it is also in the form of previous state of the effect. As for example, the pragabhava of a pot is not merely its previous absent state, but it is also in the form of a clay-bulk. So just when the form of the pot comes into existence their does not remain now the form of the clay-bulk i.e., bulk-form is destroyed, and pot-form has come into existence. Similarly when a *bhavya jiva* acquires salvation form, he loses the form of worthiness for salvation.

Why does not the *Saṃsār* become empty of *Bhavya* Souls?

Question: If the bhavya *jivas* go on attaining *mokṣa*, why should that day not come when the *saṃsār* should be totally empty of *bhavyas* just as when even one grain after the other is taken out from a store-house of grain a day comes when the store-house becomes totally empty of grains.

Answer: No, the amount of *bhavya jivas* is infinite like time. Even though, time is exhausting second by second it does not come to an end. In the same manner, *bhavya jiva* cannot be exhausted even though atleast one *bhavya jiva* attains *mokṣa* within every period of six months.

Question: Time is not limited whereas the *bhavya jivas* are limited. There is only a definite amount of *bhavya jivas* in this world. New *bhavya jivas* does not increase. So on the passing of infinite time all the *bhavya-jivas* should attain *mokṣa*, and the world should be void of *bhavya-jivas*.

Answer: No, if you count from today, upto some future infinite point of time, then that time is limited only, owing to two extremes of time being fixed whereas the past time has no beginning and so it is limitless. Now you think over this, what work of 'being completely exhausted of *bhavyas*, has not happened in that limitless past time, how can it happen in the future limited time? Whenever this question is asked in the future, 'how many jivas have attained *mokṣa* till now the answer will be one and the same that "jivas, only in an infinitesimal part of the infinite number of one *Nigod jivas*, have attained *mokṣa*". Like the other statements of the omniscient, even this statement also has to be believed to be true, by having faith in him and on his words.

Question: Why are all the *jivas* not attaining *mokṣa* not styled as '*abhavya*?

Answer: The term '*bhavya*' does not mean a *jiva* that will necessarily attain *mokṣa*, but it means a *jiva* who is worthy of (eligible for) attaining *mokṣa*. In other words, those *jivas* only are *bhavyas* who can ättain *mokṣa*, if they obtain the means of mokṣa such as non-violence, austerities and self-restraint etc. They should not be called (termed) as '*Abhavyas*' simply because they did not get these means. If the wood eligible to become an idol did not receive all other means required for the creation of an idol, then the idol will not be created. But simply because of such creation not happening in the absence of other means, wood will not be considered ineligible and unworthly for idol.

Question: If *mokṣa* is a created thing, then why should it not perish inasmuch as that which is created is destroyed?

Answer: Just as *'Dhwamsa'* (absence in the form of destruction) after being created does not get destroyed similarly *mokṣa* also does not get destroyed. Really speaking for *mokṣa* what is that thing to be created? *Mokṣa* salvation is simply nothing but the manifestation of the pure form of the soul. When a pot is broken, the *'ghatākṣa'* (sky-part occupied by the pot) is destroyed, but on account of it, there is no additional increase in the sky. In this manner by the complete destruction of all the *karmas*, the embodied soul does not continue to exist in that state; but the pure soul does exist, and now there will never be new entrance of *karmas* in the pure soul which might be subject to destruction later.

After *mokṣa* is attained, even though the soul and *karma*-particles continue to exist in the universe yet in the delivered soul there being the absence of activities of the mind, body and voice, *karma*-particles are not ever captured in that case which can bind the delivered soul. So there never arises any bondage of *karmas*. In the same manner, when there is no seed of *karmas*, how can there be any sprout of rebirth? The soul is permanent in the form of *dravya*, but transient in the form of *saṃsārik* modification; and when just the *saṃsārik* modification ends, then and there the salvation, modification starts, viz. the soul gets created in the form of an imperishable salvation-modification (*avinashi* i.e. everlasting *mokṣa paryay).*

Thus the soul is both permanent and transient. Now you cannot say that because the soul is permanent and formless like sky so it should be pervasive (pervaded) everywhere. Because first, the soul is not absolutely permanent; and second, the soul is a doer, enjoyer and seer etc. By this its all-pervasiveness is negated. Therefore, after all the *karmas* are destroyed, just as the soul attains a new modification of perfection, so it attains now the modification of naturally rising upwards in the sky. Hence it can go upto the *lokānta* (the top of the Universe). If it might be all-pervasive, where is the question of going? After it reaches up the lokānta, then there will not be such causes of downfall as *karmas*, endeavour, attraction, repulsions, heavyness etc. Therefore, it can never fall in *Saṃsār*.

Question: Why is not the formless soul, like sky, devoid of total movement?

Answer: As opposed to the sky, just as the soul possesses consciousness and the capacity for endeavouring as special *dharmas* or natures, in the same manner, the capacity to act and move is a special feature of the soul. Though in the physical actions, the soul possessing *karmas* is the cause, and along with the bodily activities, the soul is active. After all the *karmas* are destroyed, the soul on account of its previous endeavour, soon after the burden of its *karmas* is removed, attains an upward motion upto the *Siddhashilā*. But not beyond it. It is like the scoped gourd covered outwardly with clay lying at the bottom of water and coming up as soon as the clay-covering being washed down by water is removed, it acquires naturally an upward motion but only upto *Siddhsihilā*. Further, since in the *Alokākāṣa* there is no *Dharmastikāya* which is a helping medium for motion, there will not be further movement. In the *lokānta* where the soul now stays for ever, during that stay *karmik* body and bodily actions do not exist. Therefore the soul does not possess at that level, actions like movement.

Question: What is the proof of the existence of *aloka, dharma*, *adharma*, etc.? (*Aloka* means the sky beyond the universe '*dharma*' '*dharmastikāya*' means a substance helping motion and '*adharma*' means a substance helping rest, standing still.

Answer: The word *loka* is a pure word with a clear etymological derivation. Its opposite is the '*aloka*' just as inanimate is the opposite of animate.

Question: Can we believe that a pot, a cloth etc., also are '*aloka*'?

Answer: No, the opposite point of view should be in consonance with it. Just as when we say this is not a scholar; this statement of absence of a scholar is only with respect to a conscious animate individual, not with respect to an inanimate pot. In this manner, the '*aloka*' existing as a separate *ākāṣ* is proved by the existence of the '*lok*' which is *akāṣ,* and which is congruent with it. The *dharmastikāya* and the *adharmastikāya* are proved to be existent on the ground of differentiating *lokākāṣa* and *alokākāṣa*. The *dharmastikāya* is a formless substance pervading only that much portion of *akāṣ* (sky) which is called '*Lok*' *ākāṣ*; and it helps souls and matter in the movement of going etc., Consequently souls and matter can move can go up to the edge of *dharmastikāya* and *lok-ākāṣ*. Now if there did not exist this substance like *Dharmastikāya* the *jivas* and the *pudgals* would have got scattered in the boundless *ākaṣ*. Consequently, how can bondage, *moksa*, joy, sorrow, roaming in *saṃsār*, be possible in the *jivas*? Like the water helping fish in the movement in the water, *dharmastikāya* remaining only in *lokākāṣ* helps *jivas* and *pudgals* in the movement only in the *lokākaṣ*. Just as the movement of fish is favoured by water, the movement of *jiva* and *pudgals* is favoured by *dharmastikāya*. From this, *dharmastikāya* is proved to exist. Similarly the standing or staying is favoured by '*adharmastikāya*' just as an old or a sick man stands on a road supported by a stick, by this *adharmastikāya* is proved to exist.

The Existence of Mokṣa has no beginning

(It is existent from the Times Immemorial)

In *mokṣa*, infinite souls co-exist.

Question: From when did the possession of body start? From when did the existence of time start?

Answer: They have no beginning. They have been going on from times immemorial-infinite time.

Question: When did the process of attaining *siddhatva* (perfection) begin.

Answer: It has no beginning. So uptil now infinite souls attaining *siddhatva* have reached to and stayed on *siddhashilā*.

Question: How did they co-exist there in a limited area?

Answer: Even in the limited area, the radiance of thousands of lights get mingled and co-exist. When it is so, in that realm of perfection, infinite number of formless *siddha*-souls can co-exist. What wonder is there in this?

That soul which is devoid of three *guṇas*–*sattva-rajas-tamas*, and *Karma* particles, and is pervasive through knowledge is not bound. This statement is made with reference to *siddhas*.

After being thus convinced of the truth by the Bhagavān's explanation, Mandit also became a disciple of the Bhagavān along with his three hundred and fifty pupils.

7
THE SEVENTH GAṆADHARA: MAURYAPUTRA

ARE THERE REALLY CELESTIAL BEINGS?

The seventh Ganadhar, Mauryaputra arrived. His doubt was "whether the deities and the heaven exist or not". The Bhagavān says to him,—'को जानाति मायोपमान् गीर्वाणान् इन्द्र-यम-वरुण-कुबेरादीन्' । 'स एष यज्ञायुधी यजमानो अञ्जसा स्वर्गलोकं गच्छति' ।।

Because you have found these two kinds of contradictory Vedic statements, you have entertained the doubt whether deities (celestial beings) exist or not? 'Who has seen the deities who are like magical and mesmeric beings?' In other words, from the first Vedic statement one seems to feel that there are no deities and no heaven. The second Vedic statement says "those who have performed *yajnas* (sacrifices) attain heaven; because *yajnas* work as weapon and they tear off the cover of sins." From this statement, you get the idea that heavenly beings do exist.

The absence of heavenly beings is assumed because the inhabitants of hell being dependent cannot come to this world; but heavenly beings are deemed to be free and independent to come to this world, so if they really exist why do they not come here?' Since they do not come, this shows their absence.

But these are the proofs of the existence of heavenly beings:

1. Here in the *samavasaran* (the preaching-castle), the celestial beings are directly visualized.

2. The *jyotish-vimāns* (planes) are a locality, and so like a mansion, they must be the abode, the residence of some beings. These residents are a class of heavenly beings. These abodes are called *vimāns* (Planes) because the *vimāns* are studded with gems and they regularly travel through the sky in a fixed manner. Winds, clouds, a ball of fire etc. are not made of gems. So they are not the residence of any beings.

Question: Why should we not call it an illusory structure?

Answer: If you believe them to be illusory, even then the heavenly beings are proved to exist. Who can construct such illusory things! This kind of construction is beyond the capacity of human beings.

3. Just as *jivas* experience the fruits of an intense kind of sins committed by them on going to hell; similarly 'who are to experience the fruit of the loftiest kind of *punya* (good deeds?) Say, only deities. Man whose body is made up of foul smelling substances and who is subject to the afflictions of old age and disease, cannot be called the enjoyer of the supreme kind of felicity.

4. Even from the statements made by those who remember their previous births, the existence of heavenly beings is proved just as we can get knowledge of the countries and the people and places from the travellers who visited those countries.

5. Our aspirations are fulfilled by means of the adoration of *Vidya-Mantra*. That happens only by the grace of heavenly beings, just as a king's servants' aspirations are fulfilled by the grace of that king.

6. Sometimes some human beings speak in a strange manner or make strange actions. They do not speak or act thus when they are in a normal condition. So it must be be accepted that this kind of impossible like distortion takes place because of the entrance of a deity (heavenly being) into that human body. Just as a mechanical vehicle going at a normal speed in a particular direction, when takes a strange turn, and when it so happens there is the inference that 'not the machine itself, but the person sitting in it has brought about the change'. In the same manner, a heavenly being that captures a human body makes the human being act in an abnormal manner.

7. Sometimes, miracles occur in temples. Human beings get special dreams, they get special revelations. All these things prove the existence of heavenly beings, who impel them.

8. The word 'deity' is a pure word with a clear etymological derivation. Therefore, it is necessarily

meaningful. The deity denoted by this 'Dev' word must exist.

Question: The word 'deity' can be applied to a very affluent person possessing a lot of paraphernelia. He can be called a deity. Is that not so? We say to someone "Friend see! he is like a deity".

Answer: First, a word denotes prominently an existent object. Then this word is subordinately used elsewhere for attributive denotation; and it is a duplicate of the basic thing. If the denoted subject of the basic word itself is not existent at all, how can there be an attributive simile? Since a lion exists, we say a brave and courageous man a 'lion-man' '*narsimha*' that is a man like a lion.

'Dev', 'Amar', 'Girvan', 'Divaukas', etc. are independent alternative names, other words. They are not for mortals but for deities. If deities were there such austerities as penance and benevolence etc. become fruitless! If there are no deities, the Vedic statements that mentioned *'soma', 'yama', 'suraguru* etc. and the vedic statements inviting the heavenly beings like Indra, will have no meaning at all.

The Reasons why Celestial beings do not come here:

1. The transition of divine love;
2. Divine sensual cravings and attachments;
3. Infinite divine duties (like a polite person absorbed in some extraordinary duties and endeavours);
4. Independent duties liek those of men (like a *yati* who has renounced wordly life);
5. The unbearable smell of the human world.

Yet the Reasons for the coming of Deities: Here

1. The celebration of the *JIN KALYANAK SAMĀROH* (celebration of crucial events of the Tirthankar);
2. Removal of doubts:
3. Deep attachment for some one;
4. The fulfilment of a promise to carry out awakening etc.;
5. Enmity;
6. Curiosity;
7. The attraction of the spiritual strength of a *Mahātmā*;
8. The spreading of *Mahātmā's* glory;

9. Bestowing grace on friends or children;
10. Testing *sadhus* etc.

For these reasons, deities come to this world. The introducton of deities as being 'illusory' is to indicate that if even divine prosperity is transitory, what to talk of human prosperity why should we indulge in their deep attachment?

This explanation cleared the doubt of Mauryaputra and he accepted the *Charitra-diksā* at the feet of Shri Mahāvīr Bhagavān with his three hundred and fifty pupils.

8
THE EIGHTH GAṆADHARA: AKAMPIT

DOES HELL EXIST?

Now the eighth brahmin by name Akampit arrived. The Bhagavān said to him, – 'You have found in Vedas these two contradictory statements':

(i) "न ह वै प्रेत्य नरके नारकाः सन्ति" ।

(ii) "नारको वै एष जायते यः शुद्रान्नमश्नाति" ।

It means: (i) In the next life there is no hell nor are there inhabitants in hell. (ii) Those who eat food of *śūdras* (men of the fourth caste among Hindus) go to hell. Since you have found these contradictory statements in the Vedas, you have entertained the doubt whether there are inhabitants of hell, in the next life, or not?

The belief that there are no inhabitants of hell has arisen because the abodes of such deities as Chandra (Moon etc.) are visible even now; while the inhabitants of hell are not. How can we even infer that there are inhabitants of hell who are totally different from heavenly beings, human beings, animals and birds?

These are proofs of the existence of the Inhabitants of hell

1. Just because only you cannot see them you say that there are no inhabitants of hell? If so, then even there are objects like lions and tigers not seen by you...Does it mean that they do not exist? It is not true that "what is perceived only by the external senses is directly perceptible?" because by the direct perception (*atma-pratyakṣa*) *narakas* are visible to the omniscient directly.

Thus that which is known by the senses is not called in fact 'directly visible (tangible) and existent substance, because even after the activities of the senses end, the substance continues to exist. Thus the senses can perceive only a very small aspect of the nature out of multitudinous and infinite natures of a substance. When that is so, how can that be called the precept of the substance arising through a *'hetu'* (an indicator). As for instance, the inference can be this is a pot, because in the past a trustworthy man indicated such a thing is called a pot. It does not come to our notice, on account of too much of practice as we are making inferences (we need not remember the indication) but it is not direct perception. The knowledge arising through other external factors, except the soul, is in fact not direct perception (*pratyakṣa*) but is *parokṣa* (indirect knowledge). The *'kevaljñāni'*, omniscient can see directly the inhabitants of the hell.

2. Where are the most serious sins punished? Where are the fruits of extremely horrible sins to be experienced? Not in the incarnation of animals, insects, etc. because no extreme and severe punishment is experienced there. They get pleasant air, water, light, shelter in the shadows of trees, food and other pleasures. Where there is not the least of such pleasures, but where there are the experiences of only tortures like being cut, torn, pierced, burnt, baked and beaten on rocks, etc., who are such souls? The answer is that such are only the inhabitants of hell who experience these agonies.

3. In normal life a person who commits one murder is hanged but only once, but a person who commits thousands of murders where is the punishment in proportion to the offence committed by him? We must say that only hell is such a place where sinners do not die even after being cut to pieces. Again and again the limbs are cut to pieces out of their bodies, they unite and assume their original form, and they have to experience again the torture of being cut to pieces, being pierced again and again.

4. The reasons for uttering a lie are fear, attachments, hatred, illusion and ignorance. They are not present at all in the *(sarvajna)* an omniscient. He need not utter lies. So, how can the statement about hell existing in reality given by such an omniscient be false?

Then "there is no hell in the next birth" what is the meaning of this vedic statement? It only means that an inhabitant of hell after death does not again become inhabitant of hell in his next birth.

This explanation given by the Bhagavān cleared the doubt of Akampit and he with his three hundred pupils became a disciple of the Bhagavān.

9
THE NINTH GAṆADHARA: ACHALA BHRATA

'DO GOOD FORTUNES AND MISFORTUNES EXIST?'

The Bhagavān said to Achalbhrata, the ninth Brahmin पुरुषैवेदं ग्नि सर्वं.......

Whatever exists is *puruṣa* (soul). On account of this statement you have entertained a doubt regarding the existence of *punya* (good fortune) and *pāpa* (misfortune).

There are five alternative opinions regarding *punya* and *pāpa*.

(1) Only *punya* (good fortune) exists; not misfortune *(pāpa)*.

(2) Only *pāpa* exists, not *punya*.

(3) *Punya and pāpa* remain only mixed giving mixed joys and sorrows.

(4) They remain independent and give separate fruits like joys and sorrows.

(5) There is nothing like *punya* or *pāpa*, it means neither *punya* nor papa exists, and joys and sorrows arise naturally.

Of these in the first alternative the question arises; "when only *punya* exists, how can the soul suffer sorrow?" The answer to this question is: As in the case of an agreeing diet joys appear when *punya* is ascendant, and sorrows appear when it declines; whereas in the second alternative as in the case of eating unwholesome diet, when misfortune increases, sorrow also increases; and when misfortune declines, sorrow also decreases and joy takes its place. In both the alternatives, after *punya* and *pāpa* being completely destroyed to extreme extent, *mokṣa* salvation is attained. In the third alternative if the amount of *punya* increases it is called only *punya*. In the same manner, on account of the increase of the amount of only *pāpa*, the opposite thing happens that it is called *pāpa*. In the fourth alternative, joy and sorrow are not experienced at the same time. Here *punya* and *pāpa* are to be present as separate causes for the emergence of independent effects namely joy or sorrow. In the fifth alternative, 'the air blows horizontally,' 'the fire flames go upwards, 'thorns are sharp and straight' just as all this is their nature, similarly without *punya* and *pāpa,* joy and sorrow appear on account of the nature of the strangeness of '*Samsār*'.

The first, the second, the third, and the fifth alternatives are wrong. Only the fourth one is logical, the others being illogical.

If the world is strange i.e. strange happenings are only due to nature, what is the meaning of nature? Is it the substance? Is it causelessness? Is it the quality of the substance? (This is according to what is said in the section entitled 'The Second Ganadhar'.) The summary is this. We have to believe in *punya* and *pāpa* as the causative qualities of the substance themselves with a form.

The proof of the existence of the independent punya and pāpa by two kinds of inference

(i) *The inference by the cause:* Like the effects of the seeds of grains of wheat and maize, the effects of the peculiar causes namely benevolence (charity) and violence, ought to be peculiar and particular. And,

(ii) *The inference by the effect:* Two children possess such peculiar qualities as beauty and ugliness, though their parents are the same. Behind this there ought to be different causes namely *punya* and *pāpa.*

From these two inferences the existence of *punya* and *pāpa* is proved.

(iii) Even the basic cause is in consonance with the effect. The cause of a gold vessel is gold; and the cause of a copper vessel is copper. In the same manner the cause of joys is *punya karma* (good fortune); and the cause of sorrow is *pāpa karma* (bad fortune). You have to believe that such different effects have different causes.

Why are not 'Punya' and 'Pāpa' formless?

Question: Since joy and sorrow are the moulds and modifications of the formless soul, they are formless; similarly will not the causes of these joys and sorrows namely *punya* and *pāpa* be proved formless?

Answer: The cause is not always by all *dharmas* (natures) completely consonant with the effect, nor is it completely incongruous with the effect; the cause becomes only congruent with the effect or the effect becomes congruent with the cause. If the cause and effect are congruent by all the *dharmas* (natures) which possess different natures how is it that 'one is the cause and another is the effect' and there is a difficulty in saying that they are absolutely different in all aspects. If in one, there is *vastutva-dharma*, then in the other, there would appear *avastutva-dharma*, which is always different from it. In other words then ony *avastu* will be proved to exist. Then how can there be the relationship of cause and effect between *vastu* (real) and *avastu* (unreal)?

Not only cause and effect, but all the substances in this world are similar and different and congruent and incongruent mutually. Yet, specially the principal cause is said to be congruent with its effect. This means that this effect is the (*swaparyāya*) self-modification of the cause; and (*parparyāya*) non-self modification of another cause and effect. These *swaparyāya* and *parparyāya* of cause become similar and dissimilar to and congruent and incongruent with this cause. In the current topic, the union of the *jiva* and *punya* is the cause. Its effect 'joy' is its "self-modification" and just as joy is called auspicious and good, similarly *punya* also. This is congruence. There is no rule that 'if joy is formless its cause also should be formless', because congruency is not total but it is only partial.

(a) Food etc. is the cause of pleasure, but where is it formless. It has a form. In the same manner *karma* also has a form.

Question: Then you should believe that only food, flowers and sandal paste etc. are the cause of pleasures; where is the need to believe in *karma*?

Answer: Very well, but the question is, "in some places and times the external things like food etc. are the same, yet there is difference in pleasure; why?" You shall have to say that this difference is caused only by different *karmas.*

(b) And *karma* has a form, because *karma* is the cause of the body which has a form, and cause of the accumulation of bodily strength. Just as oil which has a form strengthens a pot which has a form.

(c) *Karma* has a form, because it is nourished by flowers, sandal paste etc. which have form.

Joy Is Formless: The body has a form. Karmas are their causes.

1. What is the form of *karma?*

Question: The body etc. have form, and joy, sorrow, anger, pride etc. are formless. When that is so, how can this rule be deduced that cause is always formless or cause always has a form?

Answer: The congruent cause for the effect, viz. joy etc. is not *karma*, but the *jiva*. This of course is formless. In other words we have surely found here for a formless effect a formless cause. Now to speak of *karma*, since *karma* being a non-congruent cause, there is no difficulty in its being "with a form" like medicines increasing intelligence. Thus "*swabhāvavād*" the theory of nature has been refuted, and the '*karmavād*' the theory of *karma* has been proved.

2. Now, the refutation of the theory that either 'only *punya* exists', or only *pāpa* exists.

3. By the increase of *punya*, let there be increase of joy; likewise, by the decrease of *punya* let there be decrease of joy but how can there be excessive sorrow? This can only happen on account of the excess of *pāpa*.

The body gets strength on account of nourshing food. If there is a decrease in the nourishing food, the strength in the body decreases, this is resonable; but how does disease and agony occur? This is the reasonable consequence of increase in the unwholesome and harmful food which spoils health.

4. It is all right if a *jiva* gets a small or less comfortable or less auspicious body by the decrease of *punya*, but how did such heavy and inauspicious bodies as those of elephants or large fish or of the inhabitants of hell appear? If there is only a small quantity of gold, we may get a small vessel but it is of gold; not of clay.

5. In this manner, the difficulty arises in the case of those who believe only in *pāpa*. By the increase of *pāpa* sorrows may increase, and by its decrease sorrows may decrease; but how can pleasure increase? A small degree of sin may be the cause of sorrow, but not of joy. Let poison be of a small quanity, it cannot increase the health of the body.

The belief that punya and pāpa are combined is false

6. There is no *karma* like a combined *punya* and *pāpa*, because there is no cause that can create such a *karma*. As the cause of *karma*, we can consider the auspicious or inauspicious mental, physical and vocal *yoga* activities. *Mithyatva* etc. is contained in the inauspicious yoga. But at a time *yoga* of only one kind, either an auspicious one or an inauspicious one is present, and by this only one kind of bondage either of *punya* or of *pāpa* takes place.

Dravya-Yoga: Bhāva-Yoga; Dravya Bhāva-Yoga is not mixed

Question: Do we not see the mixed auspicious and inauspicious yogas? For example, a thought or preaching of rendering charity arose, but over-passing the scriptural method and scriptural formality; or worshipping the *paramātma* but not according to scriptural method. Are not these respectively auspicious and inauspicious *Manoyoga, vāg-yoga* and *kāya-yoga* (mental, vocal and physical activities).

Answer: No. *Yoga* is of two kinds: *Dravya-Yoga* and *Bhāva-Yoga. The 'Dravya'* means helpful substances causing yoga and the activities of the mind, the voice, and the body. These are the *dravya-yoga.* The *Adhyavasāya* (good or bad sentiments) which is the nature of yoga is the *Bhāva-Yoga.* According to the *vyavahāra-naya* (normal vision) there can be a fusion i.e., a mixture of the auspicious and the inauspicious ones in the *dravya-yoga*; but not according to the *nischaya-naya* (subtle vision). Because in the *Bhāva-Yoga* there is no such fusion mixture i.e. combination of auspicious and inauspicious sentiments *(Adhyavasāya).* Whereas here there can be only auspicious or inauspicious *adhyvasāya*. There can never be such an *Adhyavasāya* which is of both auspicious and inauspicious nature at the same time. In the scriptures *(Āgamas)* are shown two auspicious meditations viz., *dharma-dhyāna* and *shukla-dhyāna*; and the auspicious *leṣyas* (mental states viz., *Tejo leṣya, padma leṣya* and *shukla leṣya).* Two inauspicious meditations *arta-dhyāna* and *raudra-dhyāna*, and three inauspicious *leṣyas* (mental states) kriṣna-*leṣya nil-leṣya* and *kapot-leṣya,* are also described but no auspicious and inauspicious combined meditation or *leṣya* is mentioned. Even after the meditation, *leṣya* prevails. The *Bhāva-yoga* is made up of *leṣya* and *meditation.* It is not in the form of both auspicious and inauspicious together. Therefore no bondage in the form of combined *punya* and *pāpa* occurs.

There are no mixed *karmas* in *samkraman* of *karmas. Saṃkraman* means intermingling of old *karmas* into the newly being bound *karmas* of the same type. Just old *ashātā vednīya karma* being intermingled in the newly being bound *shātā vednīya karma* and getting in the form of *shātā vedniya karma.*

Question: In the *kaṛma* that is auspicious and the *karma* that is inauspicious, there is a *samkram* (internal entry and intermingling). Is this intermingling not combind *karma*?

Answer: An auspicious *karma* arises from an auspicious sentiment. The previously accumulated inauspicious *karmas* become mingled with auspicious *karma* of the same sort being earned at present. In the same manner, previous auspicious *karmas* are mingled with present inauspicious karmas.

Question: In *mithyatva mohaniya karma* what is the system?

Answer: After the bondage of *mithyatva karma* if there occurs a pure sentiment, then this *mithyatva karma* gets divided into three groups. One of them is a pure group namely *samyakatva-samkit mohaniya.* This is pure group of Samyakatva Mohaniya. Now if *jiva* further again enters *mithyatva*, that *samyakatva mohaniya* gets transformed into *mithyatva.* In this manner, *saṃkraman* does not happen between the main basic *karma prakritis* just as *vedniya karma* is not transformed into *mohaniya karma* but it happens between their subordinate forms: just as from shātā *Vedaniya karma* into *'ashate vedaniya' karma*, excepting *'Aāyushya karma.* Between *darshan* moha and *charitra-moha* karmas also '*samkraman* does not happen. Now you see that with the newly bound auspicious *karmas* like *shātā Vednīya*, the previously bound inauspicious *karmas* like *ashāttā vedanīya karma (Karma* that create disease, agony) mingle or with the newly bound inauspicious *karmas*, the previous auspicious ones mingle mutually. This appears to be a *mishra-karma* like auspicious and inauspicious both, but after mingling there remains only one auspicious or inauspicious form, not both. The *karma* that mingles disappears; and the *karma*, with which it is mingled, remains in its form. For example when *ashātā* form arises; it means *ashātā* becomes *shata*. Therefore, there is no *karma* which is a fusion of *punya* and *pāpa*.

The summary is this: *punya* and *pāpa* are independent *karmas*. If they could combine, only excessive happiness for heavenly beings and only excessive pain for the inhabitants of hell would not occur. Therefore, as the independent causes of these two are separate abundances – abundance of happiness and abundance of sorrow. So separate *punya* and *pāpa* are proved.

7. Moreover in this world we see three varieties good, evil and different from these two, namely neutral. But the presence of good or evil is not the absence of each other. Just as sweet, bitter and tasteless relish; it is not only that the absence of good is evil and the absence of evil is good but the absence of sweetness is tastelessnes also not sheer bitterness. Bitterness is an independent taste. If disease abates, health appears, but not the difference in state like strength. To get this strength separate medicine must be taken. In the absence of *'durjanatā* (ignobility) there might be *sajjanatā*, gentleness (nobility) but not a lofty kind of nobility. One who commits serious sins earns only *pāpa*, but does not earn even a grain of *punya*. In this manner, even one who executes a sublime deed earns a very great *punya*; but it is not the state that one also earns a little of *pāpa*. In the same way one who commits horrible ignoble actions and evil actions, auspicious sentiments and inauspicious sentiments etc., are not the absent forms of each other, but they are independent entities. Hence their effects *punya* and *pāpa* also are proved to be independent.

Some necessary directions regarding punya & pāpa

A *karma* that gives good fruit like good colour, taste, smell touch, etc., is a *punyakarma*, and one that gives a bad fruit, is *pāpakarma*. These *karmas* are made up of subtle material particles named *karman vargana*. Therefore, they are also subtle not gross. They are also not like minute atoms, but they are in bulks.

How karma bulks stick to the soul?

They stick to the soul which is smeared with attachments and hatred, like dust sticking to the body smeared with oil. The *karman* particles stick to the soul, except in the middle part, which is utterly pure, containing eight minute parts called *'ruchak pradeśas'*. The *karman* particles stick to the entire soul except that soul's pure area, and except the sky occupied by it. The soul and *karmas* possess such mutual relation that the soul which is the support for *karmas*, by means of its own good or evil sentiments can originate *karmas* good or evil. At the same time, these four things, the nature, the duration, the intensity in fruit, and the bulk of *karmas* are determined. The effects differ according to differences in the *'āshraya'*, refuge. For example it is observed that the same water falling from sky results in the form of milk in cows, and poison in snakes. Or the same food, according to the ability to digest results (becomes converted) into flavour, blood etc. or into excretion, urine and cough. In the same manner, an auspicious or inauspicious sentiment (feeling) converts the *karman* particles respectively into independent good or evil *karmas*.

According to the *'tatvarth shastra'*, there are 46 *karma prakritis* (forms) of *punya* good *karmas* which comprise *samakir-mohanīya' 'hāsya', 'rati', 'pumved'* in addition to 42 *punya karmas* like *shāta vedni shubha-ayushya nam-gotra.* (All the remaining eleven are in the form of *pāpa karmas* inauspicious karmas). *Subh karma* has 46 forms according to the *tatvarth-shastra.* They include *samakit mohanīya, hasya, rati* and *pumveda* in addition to 42 forms according to *karma-grantha* comprising *shātāvedanīya, shubh ayushya, shubhnam, shubhagotrta,* etc. It makes a total of 46. According to the *karma grantha, samkita mohaniya, hāsya, rati and pumveda* these four are inauspicious karmas, because they cause the *jiva* to think contrary and to resort to *mithyatva.* Of these *smakita mohanīya* makes the *jiva* commit errors like doubt in about the form of *tattvas*, in the words of the omniscient and at the basic level it is the *mithyatva karma*-particle made up of *karman pudgal.* Hence it is the form of inauspicious *karma*.

This explanation given by the Bhagavān Mahāvīrdeo brought enlightenment of truth to Achalbhrata. He too accepted the *dikśā* at the feet of the Bhagavān along with his 300 pupils.

10
THE TENTH GAṆADHARA: METARYA

IS THERE NEXT LIFE?

Now, Shri Mahāvīr Bhagavān says to the tenth brahamanda scholar by name Metarya, that on account of such mutually contradictory vedic statements, 'विज्ञानघन एव.....न प्रेत्य संज्ञाऽस्ति......' 'अग्निहोत्रं स्वर्गकामः you have entertained the doubt whether there is anything like the next life, the next birth or not?

You believed that there is no next life, No Rebirth on account of the following reasons:

1. Like the whiteness of a thing, consciousness belongs to the *bhoota-pinda* (the elemental body). Just as when a cloth is destroyed its whiteness is destroyed, similarly when the body is destroyed consciousness itself is destroyed. When that is so where remains anything for going to the next birth?
2. Even though the consciousness may be different from the body, like the flames emerging from the wood, it can be transient not permanent. There is therefore no next life.
3. Even if the soul possessing consciousness may be a permanent thing, and if it is all-pervasive then it cannot go anywhere. There is therefore no going to next life.
4. In the form of the other worlds, heaven and hell are not visible at all, then what is '*parloka*', the other world? But now consider,

The proofs supporting the existence of the other world (Next Life)

1. From the inferences already mentioned, consciousness is the nature of the different independent soul but not of '*bhutas*'— the basic elements. From the reasons like the remembrance of the previous life, it is proved that the soul has come from the other world.

It is permanent as a *dravya* (a substance, a reality); but as a *paryāya* or a modification it is a transient, conscious soul.

2. There cannot be only one all-pervasive and motionless soul, because–

(i) Due to the differences among souls of attachment and hatred, sensual pleasures and emotions, thoughts and feelings, auspicious and inauspicious contemplations, existence of hell-abiders and heavenly beings, there cannot exist in the universe only one soul but there must be different souls on account of these different effects.

(ii) Since those attributes are perceptible only in the body, the soul pervades only the body; and

(iii) The soul is proved as possessing movement because it is *bhokta* (one who experiences *karma*-fruits) and roaming in various lives is capable of movements in the four *gatis*).

3. The soul is both transient and constant

Question: Knowledge being not different from the soul, if the soul is an embodiment of knowledge, then knowledge being of creative nature, is transient and so the soul also must be transient . Then whose is the next brith?

Answer: If knowledge is different from the soul, the soul can remain permanent.

Question: But there in this condition, like that of a pure sky, or like an inanimate wood, where remains the issue of the next birth, of the pure soul different from knowledge? How can there be next birth for inanimate wood? In the permanent one if there is the capacity of doing *karmas* and experiencing their fruits, then these may go on always, but it is not so. Therefore, the soul is not permanent but transient, and when it is transient, how can there be the next birth?

Answer: In vijñān, let there be creativity, and hence let the vijñān be transient, but why should it not be permanent also?

Question: Yes. Even in the pot there is not merely transience, there is also permanence; because what is a pot? It is not merely a shape but it is an aggregate of colour, taste, smell, touch, oneness in number, shape of roundness, capacity to contain water. In the previous clay-bulk also these qualities like colour etc. existed. Only shape and capacity did not exist. It means that the pot in the form of colour etc. is not newly created but is constant; as well as in the form of new shape and capacity it is created. Here the clay-bulk is destroyed in its shape and capacity. Same pot is destroyed also in its previous attributes like blackness etc. In this manner, the pot is proved to be steady (constant) and also created. In other words

The soul is both transient and constant. In the same manner, all substances and soul also are proved as steady and transient. In this position the soul sees cloth after seeing pot, the soul itself in the form of pot knowledge is lost and in the form of cloth- knowledge is created and remains steady in the form of *jivatva*. In this manner, when a man dies and is born as a heavenly being he perishes as a human being but is newly created as a heavenly being. Of course in the form of *jivatva*, he is intact. Thus the next birth is logically established and it is reasonable, relevant, coherent, consistent and reconcilable.

All the '*sat-vastu*' (real substances) have the three attributes viz. *utpād* (creation), *vyaya* (destruction), and *dhravya* (steadiness); because what is unreal cannot be created; otherwise the unreal like 'horse-horns' could go on being created! The real substance can never be destroyed. Otherwise, gradually, all substances, might be completely destroyed. Therefore, a substance in a certain form, remains intact in a certain form and goes on being created in a certain form. The prince's beloved gold pot had been broken and transformed into small anklets for the princess. In this the substance gold is the same, but forms are three. When the same substance as a pot is lost, the prince's feeling is changed into sadness; and the same substance as a small anklet is created, the princess' feeling is changed into joy, and since the same substance remains intact as gold, the king remains neutral in his feelings. The causes of these three different feelings must be different, and they are pot, anklet and gold, which must be believed as different and intermingled in the same substance.

4. If there is no other world, the vedic statements that prescribe *agnihotra* etc. for the attainment of heaven, will be meaningless.

This explanation given by Shri Mahāvīr Bhagavān removed the doubts of Metarya and he with his three hundred pupils accepted *charitra diksā* at the hands of the Bhagavān.

11
THE ELEVENTH GAṆADHARA: PRABHAS

IS THERE SALVATION?

Shri Mahāvīr Bhagavān said to the eleventh brahmin scholar named Prabhas—

Oh you Āayushmān Prabhas (endowed with a long span of life)

(i) "जरामर्य वैतत् सर्व यदग्निहोत्रम्" (ii) "द्वै ब्राह्मणी, परमपरं च"

You have found these two mutually contradictory vedic statements: Here the first statement prescribes the duty of carrying out the *agnihotra* throughout the life; and its fruit is only *swarga* (heaven) hence you feel that there can be no such thing as *mokṣa*. Otherwise why should the *veda shastra* give such a precept of ceremonising *agnihotra* during the life-time? But 'Brahma' soul has been introduced to be in two forms, i.e. *pār* and *apār*. The *'par'* is pure, enlightened soul liberated from *samsar*. This expounds the existence of *mokṣa*. So, you have entertained the doubt whether such a thing as *mokṣa* exists or not.

The Relationship between a Substance and its Existence:

Reasons disproving salvation:

1. First if you accept the existence of the pot, "The pot soul also is completely destroyed, then who has to acquire *mokṣa*?
2. *Karma* contact being in existence from times immemorial cannot be destroyed. Therefore how can there be an end to *samsār* and salvation?
3. What is *jiva*? *Jivas* are *naraka's*, birds, animals, etc. If they are destroyed, it is to be believed that *jiva* is destroyed. Then whose *mokṣa*– the salvation?

These are the proofs of salvation–

(1) Even after a light is vanished, the minute *tamas* particles of its dark soot are present in the

atmosphere, and they can be experienced by the sense of smell. Therefore, there is no total destruction. In the same manner, even after the *jivas samsār* ends, there is not total destruction of it. If the soot is blown away by wind, or if clouds are scattered, do their *pudgals* thereby get totally destroyed? No. The moulds and modifications of *pudgals* are strange. That which is perceptible by a particular sense, after a little elapse of time becomes perceptible by another sense after a little elapse of time becomes perceptible by another sense. Salt which can be perceived by the eyes, when dissolved in water, cannot be seen by eyes, yet its changed form is perceivable by the sense of taste. In the same manner, after the attainment of salvation, the *jiva* changes its mould only but is not totally destroyed; and it can be only seen by means of *kevaljñān*.

2. Though gold and clay are bound together, they are separated by means of chemical process, and pure gold is obtained. In the same manner, by means of '*samyag darshan*' (the right faith) etc. the soul becomes pure and liberated.

3. '*Nārkas*' the inhabitants of hell, animals and birds etc., are only the modifications of the soul, the soul remaining intact all through these modifications, because the *jiva* himself assumes such forms and modifications, just like a ring or the bangle is broken, gold is not destroyed, but it remains intact. In the same manner, when the modifications such as of a *Narak*, an animal, a bird, etc., are destroyed, the *jiva* is not destroyed.

Question: On account of the contact of *karmas* the *jiva* was a worldly being. After the destruction of *karmas* why should not the *jiva* be destroyed? When the cause is destroyed, the effect also must be destroyed. Just as when the lines of a picture on a paper are destroyed, the picture also is destroyed.

Answer: Jiva is not created by *karmas*, so that when *karmas* are destroyed *jiva* also should get destroyed. *Karmas* are in the form of a cover, or an attributive substance. Therefore, just as the sun is not destroyed even though the clouds covering the sun are scattered, or, just as the space occupied by a hollow pot is not destroyed, when the pot is destroyed likewise after *karmas* are destroyed, the *jiva* is not destroyed. This is essential that even after the *karmas* are destroyed, the modifications of the *saṃsār* born out of *karma's* contact such as *nārakatva*, *Tiryakatva* (the forms of birds and animals etc.) also get destroyed along with *karmas*, but the *jiva* continues to exist in its pure nature of *jiva,* i.e. without any worldy modification like a human being, an animal etc., and it now acquires the *muktiparyāya* or the modification called salvation.

The liberated soul is not destroyable because it is devoid of variations like the pure sky.

Question: At once it may not be destroyed, but in coming time why may it not be destroyed?

Answer: The soul is permanent like the sky because it is formless. Yet, like the sky it is not all pervasive because its attributes like knowledge and pleasure are observed only through the body. So the soul must be pervasive in the body. This has been proved. In the same manner, it is not always unbound, unliberated, because it gets bound by *Punyakarma* and *Pāpakarma*. Otherwise, what is the fruit of benevolence, charity and violence? In the same manner by the separation from *karmas*, the soul also is freed from bondages.

Why is it that the soul even in *mokṣa* is absolutely permanent? It is permanent in particular aspects because its knowledge-modification changes according to the subject–modification, so the soul also in accordance with change of knowledge gets changed; hence with respect to knowledge it is transient.

Question: The attachments and hatred which are the causes for *samsār* have been in existence from times immemorial, how can they be destroyed totally? Just as you yourself say that the knowledge-consciousness has been in existence from times immemorial and it cannot be destroyed.

Answer: In this world *dharma* is of two kinds

(1) *'Sahabhu'* (natural) and (2) '*upādhi-prayojya*' (directed by a *Nimitta,* created by a cause. (i) The light in the sun is natural, and so it never perishes. If clouds spread, the sun is only covered that's all; but even if very dense and dark clouds appear and spread over the whole sky, a slight lustre remains, from which we find some peculiarity, in respect of day or night; and so we can know that it is a day, since it is different from night. In the soul knowledge-consciousness is natural *dharma* like that. (ii) Sometimes, in the *sphatik* (a

transparent stone) such colours as red and yellow are observed, but they are directed attributes by others i.e. they are *upadhi-prayojya* (acquired). It is due to *'upādhi'* i.e. red-yellow thing which is placed behind the *sphatik*. As soon as that thing is removed, there will not remain even a trace of redness or yellowness. In the same manner, in the soul attachment and hatred are not natural attributes, but are *dharmas* of this sort, viz. *upadhi*-impelled i.e. manifested by other causes. They burst out on account of the producer namely '*karma*'. Therefore, soon after *karmas* slip away, they will not remain in the least; this is logically acceptable. If it is so when '*Virāg*' the feeling of indifference towards world and sensual objects, and '*upāsham.*' the control over '*kashayas*' like anger, pride etc. When these two increase and attachments and hatred decrease, and thus when the highest level of '*Virāg*' and '*upāsham*' (pacification of *kashāyas* and ignoble sentiments is reached. Why should there not be total absence of attachment and hatred?

Question: After once the attachments etc. are completely destroyed, what proof is there to say that they will not be created again?

Answer: The deterioration i.e. variations in a substance are of two kinds— '*Nivartya*'- irremovable (those variations that cannot be wiped out or removed). Gold by the heat of fire melts. This melting is to change gold into a liquid form and this liquid form is a *'nivartya- vikār'* a removable variation, because as soon as heat disappears, this liquid-form disappears, and gold again comes into the solid form.

Wood burnt by fire becomes ash. This is called *'anivartya vikār'* (unchangeable distortion), because this ash cannot again become wood. In the soul, attachments and hatred are *nivartya vikāras* (removeable changes). They are caused by *karma-samyog* (*karma*-contact) and as long as the *karma-samyog* exists, they too exist, and as soon as *karma*-contact is removed, they too are removed. Now in the salvation-state *karma*-contact, because of the absence thereof its causes like mithyatva etc., will never be created, and so attachments and hatred also will never be created.

अशरीरं वा वसन्तं प्रियाप्रिये न स्पृशतः । This Vedic statement says that 'there is such an individual who is bodyless, who is not touched by sorrows and joys viz. who is not congruent with pleasure and displeasure. This kind of individual is a bodyless liberated soul. This also proves the existence of *'mokṣa'*. It should be remembered here that this Vedic statement should not be taken to mean that "when the body is totally destroyed, the soul also is totally destroyed, and then therefore the liked one and unliked one do not touch it. The statement should not be understood thus, because the word *'asharīri'* is not merely expresssive of absence; but just as the word *'abrahman'* refers to a man other than a brahman the word *'agras'* refers to a food of vegetable grains etc. different from cow's milk, the word *'ashariri'*, in the same manner, does not denote total absence, but it denotes an existence of a real substance. Otherwise, the statement should have contained such a word like शरीरनाशः *'Sharir-Nāśh',* the destruction of the body. If even the word like *'Abrahmans'*– a *'Nay Tatpurusha Samas'*–word also does not denote only the absence, the non-existence of a brahman, but denotes kshatriya etc., then what to talk of the word like *'Ashariri'*, a *Bahuvribi-Samās!* The word *'Vasantum'* clearly denotes the dwelling of some body. Thus the word *'asharir'* clearly denotes an existent subject. If only absence had to be taken , the word *'Sant'* would have been enough. But because word *'Vasant'* is said, the word *'a-sharir'* denotes the soul that is steady on the top of *Lokānt'* (on top of *Lokākāsh*).

वावसंतं In this word *'va vasantam'* the word *'Va'* वा denotes अथवा or it suggests that even the *Vitarāg-jiva* in the worldly state i.e., who is still in the body, is not touched by *priya* or *apriya.* Here if we take in वाऽवसन्तं *'Va-avsantam'* having 'A' after *'Va'* (with अ after वा)" e.g. "*Va-A-Vasantam*" meaning one who does not exist anywhere" in other words "absolutely destroyed" that would be wrong. Because this absolute destruction will not be congruent with what is said above that the अशरीर *'A-sharir'* is solely a *Bhāva* Padārth (a real substance) quite opposite to the sheer absence- state).

The existence of Knowledge in mokṣa:

Question: Mokṣa may be existent; but since in *Mokṣa* there are no such means as the senses to produce knowledge, there knowledge is not produced, not created. Therefore such a soul will be like an inanimate object, a non-living thing.

Answer: Knowlege is not an attribute being newly created in the soul by any means, but it is its natural inherent quality, which is covered by *avarana*' i.e., veils and the instruments like senses or the penances remove those veils partially or totally and the inner inherent knowledge is revealed to that extent, i.e., partially or wholly. When all '*āvaranas*' (veils) are destroyed absolutely by तप penances and austerities of non violence and संयम self-restraint, the infinite knowledge is manifested which is called omniscience, which manifests itself fully and forever. Therefore in *mokṣa*, knowledge as the nature of the soul flashes always in its full fledged form.

Why is Knowledge a quality of the soul?

If knowlege may not be the soul's own natural quality then what is the consciousness of the soul? Nothing. Even from the beginning the soul should be lifeless and inanimate like wood. If it is so, why is it that:

(1) Knowledge is manifested only in the soul and not in the lifeless body, or the senses etc.?

(2) Even when sometimes senses etc., are not functioning, how can knowledge in the form of remembrance happen?

(3) During discourses etc., how in the mind unseen and unheard meanings are flashing out and to whom do they flash i.e. who is the container or the possessor of these flashes?

(4) Though the eyes are the same, but if good practice say of studying the peculiarities of a diamond increases, then they are quickly observed with sharp sightedness and fine introspection. How is it so?.

Therefore it is proved that the knowledge is not the quality of the senses, but is an original inherent natural quality of the soul. Soon after all the veils completely being removed like the sun brightening full in the clear sky, the knowledge manifests itself fully in *mokṣa.* After *mokṣa* is attained if all the qualities like knowledge may necessarily be destroyed totally, realness and substancehood (i.e. '*Dravyatva'* etc.) also must be destroyed. But that doesn't happen and if they remain intact, why should knowledge, happiness etc., also not be existing intact?

How does the Knowledge comprehend all the objects?

Question: Let knowledge be there, but how can that be omniscience i.e. the knowledge of infinite objects of past, present and future infinite time?

How can there exist the knowledge of infinite objects?

Answer: This perfect natural knowledge knows all the substances (objects) accompanied with their all the moulds and modifications, existing in the *'lok'* and the *'alok'* in the three phases of time. Even if previous modifications are destroyed, then also this perfect infinite knowledge sees them in the form of past modifications, and it sees the future events in the form of the future modifications. *The nature of knowledge is to know the knowable things.* Only it knows to that extent to which the veil has been removed. When all the veils are removed, then what is the obstacle there to obstruct knowing i.e. having the knowledge of all the knowable things? Even the past is also knowable as the past. Otherwise there would be no remembrance of past events. How can it know all? Thus, just as even if the mirror is small, it can reflect all objects existing before it. Similarly for the *'jñān'* for the knowledge, whatever are knowable, it can know all of them in their totality, i.e., with all their modifications. Otherwise if a limit is prescribed that it can know only this much, not more, here 'only this much', means how much? What is the deciding factor to fix the limit that only a certain number of knowable things should be known and not more? There is no one who can decide upon the limit. So it is proved that all the knowable things are known. Thus, the liberated soul is omniscient. This omniscience by its nature goes on changing as the knowable things change from time to time, because it is the direct perception of the modifications as existing in every second and every moment and as they are changing every moment, the direct true perceptions of them also must be changing. Otherwise if the perception knowledge is steady it will be false (untrue).

How can there be infinite felicity in Moksa?

Question: Well, since there are no *pāpas* (misfortunes) which are the means of sorrow in *mokṣa,* there is no sorrow there, but the question arises, similarly how can there be happiness since *punya* (good fortune) which are the means of happiness, and the body, the senses and their objects which are the basis of happiness, are not present there at all, then the happiness also can not exist there, is it not so?

Answer: No, there in the *Moksa,* happiness is infinite, unobstructed, and incessant. Happiness is of two kinds; 1) inherent-natural, and 2) creative, which is dependent upon external objects. Let the *mokṣa* being the voidness of objects, be the absence of creative happiness, yet the inherent-natural infinite happiness, natural infinite bliss can flash in its full fledged form. Even in *saṃsār* the basis, the support of happiness is not the body or the senses or their objects, because happiness is experienced by the soul, not by the body or the senses. Therefore, the basis, the support for happiness is only the soul. Happiness is a quality of the soul. The body etc., are only the means of happiness. They are the means of happiness resting upon *'samyog'* (contact). There is no need for any means for inherent natural happiness. The felicity perpetual happiness does not depend upon contact. In *mokṣa* if a soul devoid of all *karmas* can exist, why cannot as its inherent quality the bliss, the felicity also exist like knowledge? Actually, felicity is that which does not depend upon any transitory objects, but which is cognate, inherent. The soul is happiness incarnate. In *samsār* the happiness that is expecting transitory objects, changes into sorrow as soon as those objects are lost, or circumstances are changed. Therefore, the happiness of '*shātā'* (physical ease, pleasurable sensation) depending upon *punya* (good fortune) is actually sorrow; because since it is born out of auspicious karmas, when the *karmoday* stops, *shātā* disappears, and then this causes sorrow.

Question: In the same manner we can ask why is there not the converse of it? The sorrow born out of *pāpodaya* is felicity, because it depends on *karmodya*, is not it?

Answer: No, it is not so, because no person devoid of illusion experiences sorrow as happiness.

Question: In that case, then in the contact of desired objects the experience of happiness also is not devoid of illusion?

Answer: No, such happiness is in fact sorrow, but it appears to be happiness because of false perception caused by illusion *(moha)* and false previous impressions. This sensual pleasure is virtually sorrow because when in the disease of exema or ringworm, on arising itching sensation we scratch our body, we experience illusory pleasure in scratching, but that pleasure is not real happiness. It is merely a remedy for agony. Similarly, we experience joy in the excessive hankering for sensual enjoyments, which is really a sheer remedy of pain arisen out of hankering for sensual pleasures. When the hanker disappears, the contact of the same sensual objects does not give pleasure but pain. If we eat too much sweetmeats, then afterwards on the very sight of the sweetmeat, we develop disgust for it. It means that on the stomach being satisfied, the agony of the desire for sweets disappeared, and there happened the temporary relief of the agony. The agony is for the time being subsided; consequently the imaginary illusory joy disappeared.

Question: Whatever may happen later, but previously so long as there remains some *samyoga* (contact) or condition, upto that extent, the experience of happiness is real. Isn't it?

Answer: Those who adore such happiness will have to pray for the mouth of a pig, or an uncivilised person; or pray for the birth in the hell. Because the mouth of a pig has a certain taste, and it takes extreme delight in eating excrement. In the same manner, the uncivilised people experience excessive delight in eating meat and drinking liquor. Whereas the inhabitants of hell experience extreme delight in the state of leaving hell. If you choose it, you should enter that state and come out of it. If you say "the feeling of delight there is the mental illusion of a pig, or for the inhhabitants of hell on leaving it there is merely a deliverance from extreme suffering, but no real happiness"– if that is so, here also the case is the same. In the happiness experienced in *'vishay-samyoga'* (i.e. the contact of sensual objects) what is there excepting *'arati nivaran'* the temporary removal of the thirst of sensual pleasure? Say, that sensual delight is a sheer remedy for time-being of excessive sensual quenching. When a man sits down to eat delicious food, and suppose, he at that juncture hears the news of a great calamity, there his excited eagerness for delicious food disappears. There he does not feel even delicious food as an item of happiness.

Even the remedy of the agony of sensual desire is for the

time being. So after some time again a new desire arises, and to remove it one has to exercise new forced labour. Thus new quenches and new forced labours continue.

The happiness of *saṃsār* i.e. the worldly happiness depends on other's contacts (*samyoga*). It depends on the body, senses and their objects etc. It is not happiness. If the contacts exist, then only there is the experience of happiness; and all the *samyogas* or contacts are transitory. It means happiness is lost on the loss of *samyoga*. Therefore, the anxiety for keeping *samyogas* remains continuing, incessant. So such happiness mixed with anxiety is really sorrow.

Even from other point of view, the happiness of *saṃsār* arising from the contact of objects is really sorrow, because its result is the bondage of *karmas,* spiritual ruin, and wandering in mean births and experiencing severe agonies and distresses. As the *jivas* in the illusion of happiness, go on developing contacts with sensual objects, their hunger for hapiness also goes on increasing, and following this hunger they also indulge in this great lust and great sinful activities. Hence they invite for future a series of inauspicious births full of sins and sorrows. To call this kind of happiness a 'happiness' is like treating poisoned sweets as sweets.

Since this happiness of worldly objects is artificial, unreal, illusory happiness, there must be somewhere the existence of real, true happiness. Since worldly happiness is untrue and dependent on contact, the real and independent happiness also must exist somewhere. Without the original, there can be no duplicate. Without the primary thing, there can be no secondary thing. Because a real lion exists we call some human being a lion.

Question: If there are no sensual objects in *moksa,* how can there be happiness?

Answer: By this question, you mean that happiness lies in sensual objects, and that the happiness increases on the increase of those objects. In other words you conceive a ratio between the sensual objects and the happiness. But it is a wrong concept, because as an example, if you have a hunger to eat only two sweet breads but the host insisted and you ate up four breads, then there even though the happiness-container sweet breads have increased, happiness does not increase. On the contrary agony is experienced there, only sorrow is experienced. Therefore, where did lie the ratio between the sensual objects and the influence of their pleasure? On the contrary, the *munis* (Jain ascetics) who are freed from such contacts, experience great felicity. Hence after all *karma-samyogas* are destroyed, why cannot there be experienced infinite happiness?

Felicity like knowledge is a quality of the soul. Therefore, just as after the veils over knowledge are destroyed, infinite knowledge is manifested. In the same manner, after the destruction of *'vedanīya' –karma* infinite felicity is disclosed. It is not newly created like *shātā* a physical ease, but it is the nature, a natural quality of the soul revealing itself. Therefore, it is eternal.

अशरीरं वा वसन्तं प्रियाप्रिये न स्पृशतः— This Vedic statement says that the impact of *priya* and *apriya* is prohibited in the pure soul (brahma). This *priya-apriya* are in connection with the sorrows and joys dependent on *punya* and *pāpa*. In other words such joys and sorrows do not exist in *mokṣa*. They are only prohibited there by these vedic words, but this prohibition is not in connection with the eternal and natural felicity. In the phrase "जरामर्यं वा अग्निहोत्रम्" the word वा indicates that only those who desire heaven may do so. But those who desire *mokṣa* should not do so. If it were a direction for all, the word वा would not have been used there.

The summary is *'mokṣa'* exists, and it abounds in infinite knowledge and infinite felicity. The liberated soul eternally stays at the top, at the *'lokānta'* i.e. at the top of the universe, and becomes steady there for ever.

This explanation of Shri Mahāvīr Bhagavān cleared all the doubts of Prabhas and he with his three hundred pupils received *diksā* at the feet of the Bhagavān.

All the eleven brahmins after becoming *munis* salute the Bhagavān and politely ask, three times, "Bhagavān! What is *tatvam* (the extract of existance)?" and the supreme guru of the world, worshipped by all the kings of deities, Sri Mahāvīr Pramātmā answered the three questions respectively saying 'उप्पन्नेइ वा, 'विगमेइ वा' 'धुवेइ वा' – "everything is created". "It is destroyed." "It remains steady." Pondering over these three answers through three factors i.e.

i) The answer uttered by the omniscient Mahāvīr Bhagavān himself.

ii) The ripening of the *punya* namely the *'Ganadharnām karma'* earned in their previous birth, and

iii) The intellectual – potentiality called *autpatiki* (spontaneous flash of) talent etc. on account of being equipped with these three means, the *jñānavaran karmas* achieved excessive *khshayopsham* (partial destruction) and then and there all 11 Ganadharas composed the *Dwadashangi Āgam,* main 12 scriptures abiding in all *tattvas* (essentials) and the 14 *Poorvas* (Shastras) contained therein. The Bhagavān bestowed his blessings throwing on their heads scented powder of sandal wood etc. testifying to their truth and directing them to teach others. Thus the eleven brahmin *munis* became Ganadhar *Maharsis.*

This book has been written so that people may read it and understand the meaning of the *tattvas* relating to the soul, the *karmas,* the five elements, next birth, bondage, deliverance etc. and so that they may realise the true phenomenon of this Universe, may cultivate the trust (सम्यग्दर्शन) and may make endeavours to attain the liberations from *samsār.* No doubt with this auspicious desire, this book has been written, yet on account of intellectual inadequacy if something is said in this book contrary to the *jiñājna* (the words of the omniscient) the author seeks pardon – *"michchhami dukkadam".*